SOCIAL MEDIA MARKETING 2019

Use the newest successful strategies to mastery the best channels through Youtube, Instagram, SEO, Facebook and LinkedIn - Skyrocket your Personal Brand

Blake Davis

Copyright © 2019 Blake Davis

professional licensing, business practices, advertising, and all other aspects of doing business in the US, Canada, or any other jurisdiction is the sole responsibility of the purchaser or reader.

Table of Contents

Introduction

Social media, which relates to the sharing of information, experiences, and viewpoint throughout community-oriented websites, is becoming increasingly symbolic in our online world. Thanks to social media, the geographic walls that divide individuals are crumbling, and new online communities are developing and growing. Some examples of social media include blogs and vlogs forums, message boards, picture- and video-sharing sites, user-generated websites, wikis, and podcasts. Each of these tools aid communication about ideas that users are ardent about, and connects like-minded individuals throughout the world.

According to Universal McCann's Wave 3 report, released in mid-2018, social media is rising and it seems unstoppable. Amid all Internet users between the ages of 16 and 54 globally, the Wave 3 report suggests the following:

- 794 million users watch video clips online

- 746 million users read blogs

- 721 million users read personal blogs

- 707 million users visit friends' social network profile pages

- 703 million users share video clips

- 602 million users manage profiles on social networks

- 648 million users upload photos

- 616 million users download video podcasts

- 615 million users download audio podcasts

- 584 million users start their own blogs

- 683 million users upload video clips

- 560 million users subscribe to Rss feeds

Social media insertion seems to be a continuing trend. Social media marketing (sometimes referred to by its acronym, SMM) helps service providers connecting , companies, and corporations with a broad audience of influencers and consumers. Using social media marketing, companies can gain traffic, followers, and brand awareness - and that's just the beginning .

History of Social Media Marketing

Social Media seems to be a new trend, but its birth stretch to the beginning of computer era. What we actually see today is the result of centuries-old social media development. Usernets, which was launched in 1979, was the first ancestor of social media, and the journey from Usernets to Facebook is a long one. Usernets helped users to post on newsgroups. It was followed by bulletin board systems (BBS) which allowed users to login and collaborate. Online platforms like progidy were the precursors to BBS. After online services, internet relay chat came into light which gave way to instant messaging.

In the 90s, dating sites and seminars were on peak, which led to the augmentation of social networks. But they did not let users make friend lists. Six degrees launched to overcome this feature. It allowed profile creation and listing pears. It was aquired and shut down after playing for a decagon. Blogging emerged in this phase, creating a passion in social media. It is very popular even today. Other sites like BlackPlanet (African-American Social Website) and MiGente (Latino) trimmed off having provision to create profiles and add friends.

State of the art social networks came into picture post

2000. Apple launched its Friendster in 2002. It has lots of users. Hi5 and Linkedin were launched in 2003. Linkedin is a place for professionals to reach out to one another. MySpace also originated in 2003 and became well known by 2006. Similarly Facebook was commenced in 2004 and surpassed MySpace, Orkut, Multiply, etc., and is still expanding. These years also conceived media sharing platforms like photobucket, flickr, youtube, instagram, etc., along with news and bookmarking platforms like Digg and Delicious.

Since 2000, Social Media has prospered to horizon and is still prospering limitlessly. Along with media sharing, many other portals that provide real-time updates were suggested for example, Twitter, Tumblr, etc. In 2007, Facebook launched its advertising system. The gravity of social media is undebatable. It is a potent channel of marketing − a game changer for any business. It provides us the resilience to impart at both personal as well as business levels.

Field owners can improve search rankings, leads, sales, and traffic using search media. This can be done at reduced marketing costs. Besides business, it is a cool platform to associate with friends and dear ones.

Where We Are Now

Until recently, the Internet was predominantly an explanatory medium. Notwithstanding, in the last couple of years, the Internet has become progressively social. We are now looking at websites, obsessions, and demeanors of our peers in order to make well-informed and well-read findings about our next move, be it a buying decision or another sanctioned article to read late at night. Websites such as MySpace and Facebook have turned up to make communication between peers fast and easy. Social websites have been created to unify individuals with similar interests: social news sites that are governed by the "wisdom of crowds," social bookmarking sites that allow individuals to identify websites that a large number of people have already discovered, and alcove social networks that consolidate individuals under a common interest. As such, a new discipline, social media upturn, also called social media marketing, has developed.

What Is Social Media Marketing?

Social media marketing is a process that legitamize individuals to endorse their websites, products, or services through online social channels and to communicate with and tap into a much larger neighbourhood that may not have been available via long-established advertising channels. Social media, most first-foremost, accentuate the unified rather than the individual. Associations exist in peculiar architecture and amount throughout the Internet, and people are talking among themselves. It's the job of social media marketers to advantage these communities properly in order to adequately communicate with the community shareholders about relevant product and service contributions. Social media marketing also requires listening to the communities and establishing relationships with them as a representative of your company. As we will discuss later in this book, this is not often the easiest feat.

In essence, social media marketing is about listening to the community and responding promptly but for many social media business makers it also refers to reviewing content or finding a notably useful piece of content and promoting it within the vast social sphere of the Internet.

Social media marketing is a newer peripheral of search engine marketing, but it is really in a class of its own. It doesn't mean only searching; it relates to a broad class of word-of-mouth marketing that has taken the Internet by its horns. Fortunately, the anomaly is only growing at this point. At last social media marketing can achieve one or many of the goals listed in the following sections.

This book will help you not only understand the culture-shifting philosophies that make up marketing in the social media world, but also the strategic reasons social media marketing is used for business. It will;

- Help you grasp what social media can do for your business

- Help you determine what you want it to do for your business

- Show you how to calibrate what it can do for your business

It is not an establishment to social media, but to social media marketing blueprint. It peels away the touchy-feely advancement of early evangelists and gets down to business, because you are a businessperson. You don't have time for levity, games, and all that gibberish. You need to know the time and money you spend on social media is performing something for you. You need the nonesense take on social media marketing.

Why Social Media Are So Important Today

For years running a business was not so simple - you had a store or office, went to work each day, kept everything running, printed flyers or brochures to promote your business and used your profits to pay your employees and bills.

To do business in the 90' you probably needed a Fax machine and a newspaper ad, to do business in the 2000's you needed a website and a mobile phone. All you need to do business in this decade you need a Blog and Social Media. With the arrival of computers and the internet things have changed dramatically and if you want to be a presence online then social media really is that important.

These days it's very easy to start a business. In some cases depending on the type of business it is, you can be up and running on the net in a couple of hours and many of today's businesses are run solely online. For many small business owners, an online business is a fantastic way to build their business, while keeping overheads low. E-stores for example, allow people to store all their stock at home and employ maybe one or two people to arrange packaging and postage - far cheaper than renting a warehouse and an office for admin staff.

In today's tech-savvy world it pays to use as many outlets as you can to build an online presence. Whether you want to believe it or not, the majority of your customers, clients and competitors are online and unless you're there too, you're losing money.

Social media networking sites such as Facebook, Twitter, LinkedIn and YouTube give you the opportunity to reach a greater audience and to connect with your customers and clients in ways that simply weren't possible ten years ago.

We all know that creating and maintain relationships with customers is the key to a successful business but prior to now we had only distant tools to maintain and build these relationships. In the past we've had the phone, recently email and text messaging but these are one-to-one communication mediums. With Social Media we can still have this one-to-one conversations but now we involve others in the same conversation. This is very powerful from a marketing perspective.

I know that I are more likely to purchase something if it's

recommended by a friend rather than if I simply saw an ad on TV or in the newspaper. Now, you have reviews in so many different ways. By combining your website with a Facebook page, Twitter account, YouTube Channel, Blog and information-rich articles, you can not only increase the number of people who know about your business but provide them with information, discounts and promotions that you can't do with print media. And with Social Media the cost is simply your time, unless you'd like to run Pay Per Click marketing campaigns which you should.

You will find over millions of users on social media sites today, sites like Facebook, Twitter, Instagram, Facebook Messanger, WeChat, and WhatsApp have made a big impact on people's life. Not only sharing photo's and information, but trades and business have also flourished. The numbers are ever rising on the social media sites, the mass number of users on each social platform clearly indicates how important is social media in today's world, it has changed the entire concept in the field of Information and Communication.

There are several reasons why you need to be on a Social Media platform today.

Communication: Social media platforms such as

Facebook, Twitter, Google and more have made it easy to contact and get in touch anyone just by searching for their names online. Smartphones and tablets have also played a very big role, previously you needed to have a PC or a laptop, but now you can be in touch with all your friends and relatives on the move, even managing the business it's simple and fast.

You can connect with customers and clients all over the world from promoting your business and selling products to finding new clients, new media can put the world in your hands with the click of a button. And sites such as Facebook allow your customers and clients an opportunity to communicate with you, no matter where you are.

Photo sharing: With the advent of Facebook, Instagram, and Snapchat, one can now share photos about exciting moments of our lives with friends and family members miles away from us. People were deprived of such things in the past and now they are just a click away from sharing the loving moments with their loved ones sitting miles away.

Awareness Campaign: When we speak about raising funds or helping poor, social media network is always seen as a big podium to raise millions of dollars for charity or different awareness campaign such as the Boston bombing victims, where nearly about 200,000 dollars was raised.

Don't let your competition take away your business. Use social media to its fullest to create an impact online and increase your presence to customers old and new. If you want your business to survive in today's technological world you need to be where your customers are - online and on social media networking sites. Increase your presence and your business, and start your social media marketing campaign today.

Promotion: Promotion on Social Media sites has gained a lot of determination in the world of business and entertainment, people can advocate their work and increase the fan base by sharing information about their events and themselves. Through this platform, they can raise funds and transform their business in money Also, business makers can get information about what the people feel about their products through reviews.

If you've been put off using Facebook, Twitter, LinkedIn, YouTube or a Blog, you are reducing the opportunities you have to reach your customers and clients. There are still many businesses without websites, which not only makes it difficult for people to find them, but drives people to their competitors. By creating an online presence you will increase your availability to your customers and be a greater competitor to your competition.

Differences Between Social Media Marketing And Social Media Advertising

Social media marketing is the qualification to create specific plans or techniques that target social networks and applications to spread brand awareness or encourage particular products. Social media marketing barnstorm usually center around: Establishing a social media existence on major platforms. This is how you present yourself or your business to the world.

You apply social media marketing in your everyday social media posting and everything that implicates your account. This is the most important part of your journey. A successful social media marketing strategy brandish every single attitude of its profile to give users a better piece of information about your business.

First, identify who is your client . If your buyer is female, from 25 to 54 years old, based in Central London, you should put your attention on talking to this audience. What are those customers interested discover more? In this case, your market should be more abroad than when doing advertising.

- New product lines

- The benefits of using moisturizers

- New applying tecniques

- Best colors for different skin tones

- Cosmetics around the world

- Organic or cruelty free beauty products

- Interesting stories

- Makeup tutorial videos

- Cohesions with customers

A social media specialist does not need to be an expert on every topic or trend . To come up with a few of suggestions it only took me a few seconds and my experience with cosmetics goes as far as daily moisturizing. The ability or skills to understand what a costumer might desire comes from within your own company and specialists will help you to better tailor your content to fit into your business approach.

Note that the main goal with all the suggested topics is to

educate and entertain. That's the fascination of social media. It allows brands to present themselves as authority in a given subject. Once your audience follows you and applauds and respects the content you put out you are likely to have earned a new patron.

Before we get into advertising let's evaluate a proper study case. You are holder of a travel agency. You have an imminent offer for three different countries: Brazil, Greece, and Japan.

- Brazil – Summer destination, the carnival is the principal attraction. Perfect for people looking for crowded parties, beach holidays and sunny weather with hot temperatures.

- Greece – It is low season in Greece and your company wants to push packages for couples that want to enjoy quiet time in Greek heaven.

- Japan – It is winter time. Best known for its rich art, Japan is the perfect destination for a food experience , cultural shock and city holidays.

You have three very different destinations and each one of them targets a completely different type of customer. How to advertise each one of those destinations on social media? Should advertising that destination be part of your online marketing?

This is a grey area for most of the artists out there. Advertising should be developed differently from your marketing but linked to each other somehow at the end. When users follow your brand on social media they are interested in what you have to say, your approach and what your brand stands for. They are all tied to one topic and one very idea. They are all tied by the ambition to know more about your company.

If you absorb hard sell posts into your social media calendar that endorse just one of your products you will generate the consideration of only a very small percentage of your audience. Remember, your audience on social media relates to each other by a subject activity and not by a specific product. Hence among your audience, you have a very different type of people, with different interests when it comes to traveling.

When you create a post exclusively to promote one of those stations, you're subversing all the rest of your audience which is not so interested in that particular offer. The result could be repetitive and not engaging timeline of posting.

When you users realize your brand has nothing else to say than advertise its own product on social media, your brand may start losing followers and your commitment levels will drop down. And the reason is simple, your brand isn't fulfilling a need, neither is providing information and answering questions.

Your brand is only interested in selling products, making it futile for it to develop an online charisma. Users are people and they tend to connect better with other users than brands. For that reason, developing a brand personality will help your brand to bring the warmth and responsive approach it will need to allow people to connect. Once this connection is established and working you more likely have earned a new client.

Social media advertising on the other hand, is an extension of social media marketing. It works as an extra tool to help marketers to better reach their customers, spread brand alertness and promote their products. Social media advertising (SMA) cannot (or should not) exist without SMM. Although SMA is born within SMM's strategy, it has to be handled with different criterion to measure its success and return on asset. The best ways to assimilate advertising into your marketing strategy is to use your creativity in creating content at full influence.

Creativity works well within social media. It will allow your brand to talk about your products and start new conversations with your audience in an organic and alluring way. Instead of you creating a twitter post saying "Winter in Japan for "this price" you can create a blog post with the title "Japanese winter wonders". Write an article about how preposterous Japan is in the winter, what are the main appeals and why this is a great choice for your customer's next trip. By particularly writing a very explanatory article describing all the benefits of going to Japan, you are basically doing a form of advertising, totally embedded in your marketing strategy and integrated into your social media planner.

When you develop content that solves the need for a customer you are providing fair information. And, by doing that, you are automatically advertising your own product without mentioning the parts about the sales at all.

Small parts of advertising should be incorporated into your social media marketing and still provide an important source of content for your social media planners. Returning to the travel agency example, the Japan blog post will add extra value to the travel agency company, showing up on online searches as results for "travel in Japan". It will naturally reach many other users that after reading your article might have their curiosity trigged to see the offers the travel agency has to offer. This piece of content will be forever introduced on the main webpage and it's now an extra source of information about your own services.

Although it is emmensely important for your organic social media marketing/advertising, it does not represent a powerful way to increase sales and convert new clients . However, the return on investment is very positive. The organic reach of users does not require investment, leaving the only investment in this case to the creation of a content. And it will also improve your SEO rank, leading new search to the content your brand is developing . If you have a solid team that produces quality content frequently, integrating advertising in creative and sophisticated ways into your social media calendar will ignite your business online presence.

In denouement, every social media achievement should start with a well thought-out social media marketing strategy. But simply looking at a social media profile you should know exactly what that person/company is talking about . This is how you will set the tone of your online presence and tell the world what are yours abjectives. Social media marketing is the online "humanization"of your brand. This is the only way your brand carries an actual voice and participates in the public opinion. This is what brings the spice, your public is looking for to feel nothing more than entertained. The main contrast between SMM and SMA is that marketing will win new customers/followers with personality and knowledge; while advertising will fulfill a need and provide a service. Understanding the difference between those two approaches is the first step to a incredibly successful journey on social media.

Social Media Marketing Strategy

In my opinion, almost all strategic planning   try on acquiring new customers. When you take a hard look at your collective objectives, don't they always boil down to getting more people to say "yes" and buying products and services from you so your business will rise ? Internet marketing serves the same purposes and objectives . When it comes to marketing, there are three channels or lanes people will use to connect with your business.

1. **Direct or Return Traffic**. This is when an individual has bookmarked your website or has received marketing collateral (business card from a salesperson, brochure, newspaper ad, etc.), or heard about your business in some way and they visit your website. Direct or return traffic to your site should increase over time. People may become aware of your business through the other channels (i.e.: social sites or search) but when they return, they will most likely just type your website or blog address into their browser.

2. **Search Engines.** One of the most important channels to leverage for growing sales is search. In North America alone there are over 25 billon searches conducted within search engines every single month. This offers huge potential for companies who know how to become visible in this channel. That's why I dedicated a whole chapter on how to make your content as search engine friendly as possible. The visitors you receive from search should also grow over time. You'll also want the phrases that are being used to find your business align with the targeted key phrases you've used when optimizing your web content.

3. **Social Media Sites.** Social media sites such as Twitter, Facebook, LinkedIn, and YouTube also help customers find you and drive traffic to your business website. You'll develop strategies to grow followers and entice them to visit you. This traffic should also grow over time.

When your potential customers land on your page, four things could happen.

Leave instantly. Visitors can land on your blog or website, gather the information they need and exit, or they could decide that you're not relevant to what they were hoping to find and quickly leave. Think of your site as a leaky bucket. Part of developing a solid Internet marketing strategy will be to identify and monitor where the holes are within your site and plug them up with better content and calls to action. Website abandonment is when visitors land somewhere within your environment and hit the back button before clicking to a deeper page. This is also known as bounce rate. You'll want your bounce rate decrease over time.

Decide to follow you. Regardless of how and where someone finds you it's critical to make it easy for them to follow you. Make sure you have links to Twitter, Facebook, LinkedIn, YouTube and RSS feeds easily reachable on all of your Internet platforms.

Opt-in. A visitor can decide to request further information from you by filling out a form, registering for an event, or downloading value-based content. A well optimized climate should expect 2% - 10% of visitors to opt-in. There are two types of potential customers who will connect with you this way, which I discuss later in the book. For now it's important to understand that once someone has opted in, you'll need to provide them over time with useful information and multiple touches to turn these potential buyers into new customers.

Reach out to Sales. Some visitors will decide to pick up the phone and reach out to your sales department, ask a question or make a purchase. Make it easy for them by putting your phone number in a highly visible place on every page of your site, blog, and social media platform. This will prevent them from having to dig for the information and cause you to potentially lose sales. This is another area where you should see an increase over time.

When developing a social media business plan it's important to be mindful of this process and all the different ways to target and engage your audience. The best way to do this is to identify, define and document what winning looks like for your business.

Your Three-Legged Stool for Success

Any strong strategy starts with laying a solid authority and your social media marketing plan is no different. Just like with SEO 2.0, there is a three legged stool and each leg is a critical component to establish a successful strategy for your business. These three legs include characterizing your goals and objectives, measuring your performance against those goals and objectives, and then refining those goals. Let's look at each of these in parts. Just like any three-legged stool, these three elements bind together to achieve a common purpose. Remove one of these legs and the whole strategy will fall apart. You actually can't refine your strategy without measuring and you can't measure without defining what to measure.

First Leg: Define

The first step in developing a successful social media marketing strategy for your business is to identify, define, and document your goals and objectives. Over the next few pages, I outline a process and point you to resources that will help you think through this critical step in strategic planning. Begin by considering your corporate objectives. Social Media must tie into these objectives to lay a proper foundation for success. Corporate objectives represent the highest priority for your company during the next 12 months.

Business owners often struggle with differentiating a corporate objective from a marketing objective. Recently, I was training a group of business owners and I asked everyone to share with the group their corporate objectives. One member said, "To hear my phone ringing "When I asked her why did she wanted her phone to ring, she said, "Because when my phone rings I make more sales." Then I asked her why she wanted to make more sales and her answer was to be richer and I followed up with one last question, "Why do you want to increase your marketing?" Her response was perfect, "Because businesses must grow or get smaller and I want my business to rise ." I said, "Perfect! You now have your associates bjective, to grow your business. All we need to do now is figure out by how much you want to increase your business." Her answer was 50% then explained to the class that this owner had just worked out a lot of her objectives:

- Grow revenue by 50%. This is a   sort of a corporate objective

- Increase sales by receiving more calls from eventual customers. This is a marketing objective.

When you can answer the question "why?" to an objective, then you really have a lower-level objective or tactic. It turns out that "making my phone ring" was really a marketing objective, not a corporate objective. Once you can't answer why anymore, you are more than likely at your corporate objective. Push yourself to ask why until you can't anymore and this will lead to your true corporate objectives. After you've done this, we can move on to connecting these objectives to social media.

Creating Your Purpose Statement for Social Media

A key step in this first leg of the stool is to determine your purpose statement for social media. In essence, what is it you are hoping social media will do for your business? To do this effectively you'll need to connect the dots between your purpose statement for social media and your mission and value statement for your business, as well as your current overall corporate objectives. Here is a simple template to use for your social media purpose statement:

XYZ will leverage social media to [corporate objective, or element of value statement, or mission statement] in [year]. This will be accomplished by [list high level actions-these will typically center around building community, leading with value, delivering quality content, and include your high level way to convert your audience.]

Once you've written a purpose statement for social media in general, I recommend you actually write a purpose statement for each of your social media channels. For instance, how will Facebook help you accomplish that purpose statement? How will LinkedIn do that? What will

YouTube do to help your business?

Here is an example of a purpose statement for Twitter;

To increase sales by:

- Analyzing and connecting with influencers and customers

- Providing practical information to nurture relationships

- Drawing the community to our website and blog for additional information and/or special offers

This will be measured by:

- Increasing our community on Twitter

- The number of visitors that come from Twitter

- The number of Twitter visitors that respond

It will be difficult for you to accomplish if you cannot connect these dots because at some point if you can't answer the question "why am I writing this blog again?" or "why am I spending time following people on Twitter?" you'll someday give up. But if you can focus on how these actions are helping you achieve your corporate objectives, mission, and values then you'll have the perfect power needed to succeed.

Making a Comparative Analysis

As a business owner you know how much any new venture will cost you before you start to lay the foundation for a well-structured plan. The same is true for social media marketing. How would you like to put social media marketing on a quota and know exactly how many new customers you will need to produce from your efforts for social media marketing to make sense? The easiest way to accomplish this is with a provisional analysis. To come up with your social media quota, take your social media expenses, for example the dollars you're paying individuals within your organization or outside advisors, as well as, any advertising dollars you're planning to spend within the assorted social channels, and divide them by your ongoing cost per lead or precurement. For example, if you are planning on spending $3,000 per month on social media marketing and your current expense per lead is $100, you would divide $3,000/$100. Social media marketing will need to achieve 30 leads per month to be equivalent to what you've done in the world of conventional marketing.

You wouldn't be reading this book if you didn't already know traditional advertising is eroding and therefore comparing social media marketing to your previous advertising expenditures is an early stage benchmark to get a good overall picture of your future outcomes.

Who is Your Target Market?

Another key step in the Define leg is to determine your target market. When it comes to social media, your target market has a much further reach than traditional marketing, as well as different visible players. Just like in the past, your present customers are the low-hanging fruit of your marketing efforts. In addition, people who because of what they do or their interests are also potential customers for you. What makes social media marketing unique is your target market also includes influencers. These are the people who are online talking about your industry in social media and whose followers are your current and potential customers. These influencers may be partners or vendors you are currently working with who are stakeholders in the success of your business. They could also be competitors. Yes, I just said that one of your targets in social media could be your competitors. I told you early on that social media marketing is the upside-down and inside-out world of marketing.

Each of these groups is valuable to your success and it is important that you identify them in your social media business plan, understand where and how they are using social media so you can engage with them. Where are they spending time? What sites are they visiting and commenting on? This knowledge will help you manage your time as well as the content you need to create and share. For instance, if your industry and your customers are engaging on LinkedIn more so than Facebook, you'll spend more of your time in LinkedIn.

You might acknowledge breaking your target audience into primary and secondary audiences. For example, customers and prospective customers might be your primary spectators and influencers like partners, vendors, and competitors would be a secondary audience. Once you have cut them into groups, you should consider what your desired actions would be, by target audience. Actions by audience could be things like:

- Following you in your Social Media

- Visiting your websites vlogs or blog

- Appreciate and therefore likeing or sharing your content

37

- Opting-in for an event or for a specific premium.

- Requesting a quote for something or ordering a product

Identifying Social Media Profiles

There are different types of users within social media. Your target audience, regardless of whether they are customers, potential customers or influencers will utilize social media differently. Let me define the different ways people engage social media to help you understand the varying behaviors. This will help you determine desired actions by audience. Forrester Research has defined the different profiles as Creator, Critic, Joiner, Spectator, and Inactive. Let's take a look at each.

Creator: At the top of the social media food chain is the creator, which is someone who creates social media content. Creators write blogs that typically exist inside of an environment they own or control. They can also create videos or video blogs they share within their blog site, on YouTube, and as podcasts through iTunes, etc. By following the approach outlined in this book, becoming a creator is in your future.

Critic: The critic is a person who creates social media content but they publish it in someone else's environment, typically as comments to blogs or other social media content. This is a person who may not have a blog themselves but is active in others' blogs or they are commenting on seminars or even going to sites such as Trip Advisor and talking about vacation destinations, accommodations, and restaurants they enjoyed or didn't like. Critics don't just "criticize " they are primarily expressing their opinion. Think of it like a movie to be judged . You will also need to become a judge. This will be important to your success.

Joiner: The joiner is a person who has a social media profile, like a Facebook profile or a LinkedIn profile, and they update their profile periodically. These are individuals who will follow you and read your social media content. You will also be able to gain a lot of insight about what people are interested in by watching what they post.

Spectator: Spectators are people who are unquestionably involved in social media today but they don't yet have a profile and they may never have one. They're may be watching YouTube videos or they're reading blogs. They may never create social media content as a creator or a critic, but they're definitely part of your target public.. I embolden you to not forget about bystanders. Just because they don't have profiles doesn't mean you won't be able to get to them through social media.

Inactive person: This is a person who you won't be able to reach through social media because they're not involved online. A very small percentage of your target audience would hit this category so you'll have to reach them some other way.

Conducting Competitive Analysis

Another thing you need to do in defining your goals and objectives is a competitive analysis. You need to understand what your competitors are doing. Are they on Twitter, Facebook, LinkedIn, etc.? What are they saying to their target audience? What type of content are they creating? How many fans and followers, etc. do they have? A terrific benefit of social media is that it is truly open. You can easily learn from your competitors by watching and measuring them. You can find your target audience by looking at their followers. At this stage of the process, check out your active competitors and note the following:

- What social media platforms are they utilizing?

- How many fans/followers do they have?

- How much content are they producing (i.e.: number of blogs per month and/or videos per month)?

Who Are Your Contributors?

Contributors are the subject matter experts within your organization who help you create social media content. It may be you, but I hope it's not just you. I hope you have product managers, technicians, customer service people and other key contributors who can help engage in the conversation and create social media content for your company.

Second Leg: Measure

Within your social media business plan you also want to determine how and what to measure. The easiest and most obvious would be to determine and measure activity. How many blogs per month do you want to publish? How many Facebook status updates? How many Twitter posts are you going to do on a monthly basis? When we look at each of the major social media platforms, I'll give you suggestions on the appropriate amount of activity to consider. Document these in advance so you can see if you are getting off track once you begin the process. You'll also want to have results. Here are a few general social media cadences that you might consider measuring against.

1. The growth in exclusive visitors to website and blog.

2. How many contest sceptics entries you have.

3. The number of people who download or reclaim coupons.

4. The number of views of your YouTube video and total views in your YouTube channel.

5. How many times your company or products are being cited through social media.

6. The number of comments posted from the audience , either in your social media channels or on your blog.

7. How many friends, fans or followers you have.

8. How many times your post content reposted, liked or re-tweeted.

9. The number of inbound links your website or social media environment is generating.

10. The amount of inbound traffic you're receiving from social media.

All of these items can be easily measured and documented. Set goals for where you expect to be each month and compare your results with those goals. Also take a baseline of the things you can find out about your competitors. This will help you continue down the path of doing social media marketing. You'll be able to measure against where you started, where your competitors started, and how you're stacking up against their growth.

Third Leg: Refine

The refinement leg is a critical element of your strategy that will propel your social media campaign in the intended direction. By following the steps outlined in this chapter, you will develop a sound social media business plan that will serve as a road map you can measure against. This leg of the process will need to be reviewed monthly. First, you'll want to set new goals in the areas where you are exceeding initial expectations. It's important to raise the bar and push yourself further when you are achieving certain measurable targets such as cost per lead, cost per acquisition, and number of fans/followers per month, etc.

Next, take a look at those areas where you're not achieving set goals and where you're missing the mark because that will enable you to manage by exception and really hone in on certain areas of your marketing efforts. This process will force you to ask the difficult questions of why it is not working the way you had hoped, and how do I fix this. By asking yourself these questions, you'll come up with solutions and changes you can implement that will likely improve your situation.

Understand Your Audience Better Than They Do

With the great diversity of marketing styles and strategies out there, it's easy to lose sight of some of the fundamentals inherent to every strategy. Realistically, only a handful of principles are necessary for success in literally every marketing strategy out there. One of the most important is this: You have to know your audience, inside and out.

If you don't know your audience, you won't even know what strategies or media to choose, let alone what messages to give them or how to treat them once they become full-fledged customers. So let's take a look at some of the actionable, practical ways you can better understand your audience.

Do your research in advance - First, do your market research, and make sure the demographics you've selected are the right ones for your brand and product. A number of modern tools are available to help you here, some of which are free - like American FactFinder, which uses United States census information to help you find out key pieces of information about specific demographics. Don't just look at the one demographic you've assumed from the beginning; branch out to learn about related niches, and gauge interest in your product from other areas. Walk away with enough information to make at least a handful of conclusive statements about your target audience.

Look at your competitors - In some ways, this is an alternative form of market research. Here, you'll be looking at your competitors at least the ones who share the same target audience as you. Evaluate their brand, their brand voice, the types of marketing strategies they use and the messaging they bring out in their advertising. What techniques are they using? Why did they use this specific phrasing, rather than some other phrasing? This image rather than that one? There's a chance your competitors don't know what they're doing, either, but even then, you can start picking out what doesn't work, or what seems wrong and why.

Create a customer persona - The customer persona is a tried-and-true tactic used by businesses everywhere to better conceptualize their target demographics. Here, you'll work to create an outline of your ideal "target customer." In most cases, this takes the form of a fictional character, whom you shape with bits of information like education level, family life, career and income, and maybe even details like a name and personality traits. This helps you conceptualize and "talk to" your average target customer, and it serves as an ideal tool to get your other team members up to speed.

Get to know your clients personally - This is a big step, but you can only start taking it once you have some actual customers. When working with your clients one-on-one, take some extra time to get to know them on a personal level. How do they talk that's different from other demographics? What are they usually concerned about when they talk to you? What appeals to them, or scares them, or excites them? You can't always apply these insights to a general audience, but as you get to know more clients individually, you'll start to see overlap here, and then you can start making useful generalizations.

Monitor reader comments and engagements - Comments and engagements are particularly important if you're running a content marketing or social media strategy as you should be. Your goal here is to pay close attention to how many people are responding to your work, how they're responding, and how often they're responding. Generally, the more "engagements" you receive (things like comments, likes and shares), the better your campaign is faring. You can use this information to discover what content topics your audience values or what types of messages don't appeal to them. Gauge these metrics over time to establish patterns and learn more about your public .

Witness external social habits - Of course, you can also engage the tactic of social listening to see what other topics and engagements your audience members are competing in. The idea here is to "plug in" to the social conversations and engagements your target audience has with other brands and other people, giving you the convenience to divulge new trending topics, new angles for your messaging or new approaches you may not have otherwise considered.

Conduct surveys – At last we have the most straightforward way to learn more about your audience:

asking them questions. It doesn't take much to create and launch a survey, especially with a stylish tool like SurveyMonkey. Everything you want to know about your target audience, you can put in a question arrangement and submit to your social followers and email subscribers. From there, you can apparise the results (or read them manually) and walk away with all the insights you ever wanted. The only caveat is that you may have to motivate participation with a prize or reward.

All of these strategies will help you better understand your target demographics, but remember that this is still only one side of the equation. Once you know the habits, lifestyles, behaviors and preferences of your key demographics, you'll still need to mold and improve your strategy accordingly. All your insights need to have some measurable influence - otherwise, they'll stay confined to the realm of the conceptual. You need a bottom-line impact.

Repetition Is Key

Repetition is used in advertising as a way to keep a brand or product in the forefront of consumer's minds. Repetition can build brand familiarity, but it can also lead to consumer fatigue, where consumers become so tired of an ad that they tune out or actively avoid the product. Therefore, to be effective, repetition must occur in the right proportion, as too much repetition may be counter-productive as an advertising strategy.

How many times should a message be repeated for maximum effect before it goes the other way and breeds contempt? According to some studies, the answer is between three and five times

How to tap into the power of repetition to engage your audience:

Limit your messages - For the strongest impact, select a small number of messages and focus on repeating these through more frequent campaigns.

Create a plan of regular communication - Targeting your audience with one message will not yield results. Research shows consumers need to be exposed to your message at least three times before they will take action. Remember, frequency breeds familiarity, and familiarity breeds trust.

Use multiple channels - The best results come from targeting your customer across multiple channels: letterbox advertising, print, packaging, outdoor, in-store, email, social media, radio, PR and so on. Use subtle variations in your ads to recapture your audiences' attention.

Strike the right balance - What is the correct frequency for your campaigns? Take time to test and measure results so you can find the right balance.

Personal Branding

Personal Branding is a marketing strategy to make your skills stand out from other professionals in your industry. It is a system which differentiates you from the crowd and positions your work skills as superior to others.

The keyword here is standing out. When you stand out in your industry, people take note of you. They see you as a thought leader. You create a position where you can get more work and charge higher prices. Also, your network starts becoming richer.

So how do you stand out in your industry?

You do so by having a deep understanding of your target audience's needs and then solving those needs exceptionally well and in a medium they understand best. When you highlight their pain points in their own language and then deliver them an exceptional solution, you stand out. You become insanely more favorable than someone who is not establishing this empathy.

Everyone has a favourite brand - you just may not realize it. Wherever you've entered personal data, you've created a persona that makes up part of your personal brand. Add to these personas amass data like browsing history, shopping habits, and social media, and that's your online persona. Now, while you can't do much to change the data companies can gather regarding your online spending habits or the information deduced from your browsing history, you can absolutely control how you present yourself to the digital world via social media branding. By controlling your personal brand, you ensure that people see what you want them to when they Google you.

The right personal branding can help your career by helping you to establish yourself as an expert in your field, a thought leader, or an influencer. When there's a promotion on the cards or when you're actively seeking a new role, employers are likely to Google you, and if you've taken control of your personal brand, you'll dazzle them with your professionalism and your position as an authority in your niche.

What do you want to be known for? What is your ideal career, and are you hoping to move toward it? These are important questions, as without clear goals, you'll never achieve branding success, as your posts will be too scattered to be useful or influential. For example, if your long-term goal is to work as a senior digital marketer at a big brand, it's important that you join and participate in industry-related conversations and network with other influencers in this space.

Your target market feels - "Hey! This guy really gets me". From there on, they look at you as a solution to their problems. Of course, there are many strategies and tools which greatly amplify your personal brand. But at its core, it's all about understanding your audience and addressing their needs in a way no one else can.

The Importance Of Personal Branding

Personal branding has always been important. But in the age of short attention span coupled with the biggest opportunity since the dot-com boom, it is one of the most important disciplines to master for any entrepreneur or executive.

Here are some of the biggest benefits of building your personal brand in 2019:

Money - When you build your Personal Brand, your voice becomes synonymous with the voice of your industry. You are perceived as the symbol of trust, authority, authenticity, and quality in your industry. This can lead to high paying work opportunities and higher prices for your product.

Recognition - It gives you an instant recognition tool which opens a lot of closed doors and opportunities. This, in turn, gives you an instant head start over the competition.

Networking opportunities - You get to network with A-list influencers and CEOs of top companies. This allows you to make a quantum jump in your career. You are in a position to form relationships with these influential people and exponentially grow your business in a very short time.

Position - You achieve a position of power as a thought leader in your industry. Your words carry more weight. This aspect is more vanity based but great towards reaching your self-actualization goals. After all, who doesn't want to be famous and get respect from their peers?

A career full of perks - You get to speak and get invited to conferences and summits in your industry. This comes with perks like higher pay, less strenuous work, more visibility and traveling to amazing places.

Higher productivity - You become more productive and responsible. When you see the results of your hard work with people starting to notice you, you feel a sense of pride and power. These results make you more attracted to your work.

Confidence - You become more confident and it adds a positive touch to your personality. When your words and actions matter, you shed doubts about yourself very fast. You tend to become more confident and vocal. Overall you move towards becoming a wholesome personality.

Dream job - Getting your dream job becomes much easier with you being a known name in the game.

The Psychology Science Behind It

Most businesses starting out don't recognize the significance of branding in regard to marketing. Branding, to put it simply, is to give your service or product an identity; something that is recognizable to consumers and competitors. When you brand you are creating a symbol, name or design that differentiates you from the others in your industry.

This is best done through subliminal messages while still using features of marketing that subconsciously impact consumers and potential customers. Most of the prominent and successful brands you see today use psychology to impact their consumers with effective marketing material. This is achieved through using specific colors and images to distinguish their brand, promoting their services or products through promotional values, give-aways, and sales. This also heavily achieved through the use of a fabricated lifestyle framed around what they offer.

Knowing your target audience is essential to this aspect of marketing a lifestyle. The demographic plays a big role in how well your audience will respond to what you are promoting. There should be consistency within the message being sent to the target audience to plant a seed in their minds as well as create something that is memorable within their subconscious. The personal perception of the brand is the most integral part of a brand's selling power.

When you are able to create demand for a supply that isn't necessarily essential, but deemed as desired or attractive, this is the driving force behind brands that have become household names. This is also what drives the bulk of their sales. That's when you know you have reached industry leadership. When the message of a brand is perceived as something that is easily assimilated into a consumer's lifestyle, they begin to identify with the brand and become a repeat customer as a result. It is important that when showcasing a lifestyle, you fully grasp what is so appealing about it and get that across to your target audience.

Customer satisfaction can be defined as a consumer

purchasing a product that fulfills his needs and the certain amount of expectation he has for the brand he is buying. When those needs and expectations are met, this in turn creates a demand for that brand as a result and the retention of a customer for that brand. If the business is perceived as having the ability to give something to the consumer then in turn the customer gives back by purchasing. This can transform into a term called brand loyalty. Brand loyalty exists only when a consumer has a high opinion towards a certain brand exhibited through the action of repurchasing.

This translates into a cycle of repeat consumption. By appealing to potential customers psychologically, you are giving your brand the power to impact the lives and actions of those interested in what you are offering. When you foster a good relationship with customers you are feeding the process of transformation and in turn gaining more customers as a result.

There are other qualities that help shape the big players you see today, one being good quality customer service. If a business has poor customer service, 89% of people have said they would not return no matter the quality of the product. Giving consumers the ability to feel important is significant to the buying process, you must cater to their needs as they will give you what you need in return.

There is also truth to consumers associating a certain brand with a particular service based on the persona or message that brand conveys. If a brand is depicted as luxurious or elite, the highest customer service and care is anticipated to match this image. If that is not the case, this can deeply influence a consumer's perception of how legitimate or desirable this brand is to them and the general public. The opposite applies, if a brand has a customer service policy that matches the brand in question's reputation, this can do a lot for the way the brand is received by those interested in purchasing products or services from the place of business.

Another outstanding approach is using attractive ad imagery and ad copy to appeal to the target audience. The three key aspects in marketing imagery are icons, type face (font), and a color palette. People accomplice a brand and their products or services on these features. Depending on the industry your business is in, it is important to abduct the principle of what your ideal consumer would want through these factors and the image the product gives them. A study called Exciting "Red and "Competent Blue" supports the idea that acquiring patterns are undoubtly indicated by colors due to their impact on brand impression. This means colors having a role in the way consumers define a brand's persona. Based on their opinion of the brand and what it offers in terms of a persona to those wearing or using their products/services, they will assume it worthy of their purchase or not. In plain English, to articulate that they must possess this product or use this service and if they don't they are truly missing out on something that can really change. Sounds dramatic, but that is the involvement most people have with their favorite retail items and repeat services that have become habitual after a certain point of consumption.

By giving off the deception of high-demand, you are not only filtering the interest of a potential consumer, but also a sense of urgency that develops once they know they don't have that item and seemingly so many others do. Prominent demand is a great tool to use for purchasing growth. By having an aspect product and understanding the mind of the ideal customer and your wider target audience, you are able to not only attract new buyers, but keep them coming back to your place of business and make a customer for ever.

Personal Branding Strategies

We are living in the golden age of internet. Building a personal brand has never been as easy as it is now. Yet so few people are taking advantage of this brilliant opportunity which marketers of the past would have killed to get a shot at. Let's not let this opportunity slip away. Here are step by step personal branding strategies which leverage the internet to make you stand out from the crowd.

Define your target audience - First and foremost, have a clear idea about who your target audience is. What do they want in life? What are their biggest aspirations? What are their biggest fears? What are their main problems and roadblocks in overcoming those fears? Where do they hang out the most? Conduct a thorough research on all these questions and then base your message on how best you can meet their needs and expectations.

Identify and narrow down your niche - It's nice if you are a Jack of all trades, but when branding, the key is to focus on one special superpower of yours. Think of what you are most passionate about and what comes naturally to you. Once you identify that superpower, make it your niche. For example, If you have a lot of passions but overall you are most passionate about improving lifestyle, select lifestyle design as your niche. Next, you should narrow down your niche to address a specific demography. For example, after you select lifestyle design as your initial niche, you can narrow it down to address a specific community and make your brand message custom tailored for them. So instead of lifestyle design, it can now become lifestyle design for entrepreneurs or lifestyle design for single dads. This way your message comes across as tailor-made for a particular set of demography and hence more appealing to them. If you have more special qualities, you can connect them under the umbrella of your main superpower. For example, if apart from lifestyle design, you are also good in personal finance, then after creating a string of lifestyle design related content, you can connect your insights and tips on personal finance as an actionable strategy to achieve a perfect lifestyle.

Stand for something - The key to building a brand is to stand for something. Create a movement by representing something which is unique to your personality and instantly identifiable to you. Remember to always be original even if at times your opinion does not have the popular vote. Have a set of values and own them by structuring your personal brand around it. Help people self-identify with your movement by giving them a title by which they can identify themselves and other members of the community with. A great example of this is Russell Brunson and his Funnel Hacker Movement. Russell Brunson is the Founder of

ClickFunnels, a sales funnel software company. He created a movement around his brand by addressing his community members as Funnel Hackers. This gave the members something to identify with and added a sense of purpose to what they were doing. It made them loyal to the brand as they felt part of a community of entrepreneurs with similar values, ethos, and goals.

Create a Mini-Manifesto around your brand - Establish a culture around your brand by creating a mini-manifesto. This manifesto will list down all the values, mission and vision of your community in a mini-document. It will act as a rallying cry for the community and reinforce the values whenever the community is in doubt. It will show your industry what you stand for and against. This will help fellow members of the industry self-identify with your values and be magnetically pulled towards your brand.

Create a personal branding statement - A personal branding creation is your main value proposal presented in the form of a unique catchphrase. It tells your target audience (your prospective customer) what they can wish to get from your professional skills in the form of results and ultimate benefits. For example: "I help B2B companies (target market) double their leads (result) with LinkedIn ads (skill)." You can use your personal branding proclamation as part of your social media bio and as an introductory line while networking in meetups and conferences.

Create a strategic bio - How dire will it be if you win the leads with an awesome piece of content only to put them off with a crudely done bio? Your public impressed by your content will look into your bio to know more about you. Take levarage of it by crafting your strategic bio beforehand which highlights the single biggest benefit your audiences can get from you. Then engage this benefit with your superpower or special skill. The bio should contain not more than 50-60 words. Additionally, mention all your media features and showcase your worthy achievements. Influence it to the hilt by making it a common bio for your own blog and all your media columns/features. Remember that the bio should reflect your values,culture or opinions and what you stand for.

Have a brand logo - Personal branding is a process which involves both textual and visual content. Have a brand logo which assimilate the ideology and values you stand for. Create something which stands out and communicates your message visually in the best possible way.Treat the logo as more than a piece of design and more as your brand existence. Your customers will treat this image as compatible with you. So make something which represents your focus message.

Start creating content - Start a blog or a vlog based on your product and niche. Select the best keywords in your industry and start creating consistent content around it. What are the main pain points of the target audience? What are the strategies that work well in your industry? What are the latest trends in the industry? What are the popular tools to grow a business in your field? Write and make videos about all this. Put the articles in a blog and videos on YouTube and other social media channels. Above all, focus on being an evangelist of your niche to the outside world. Think what kind of information an outsider would need to get into your industry and create content around that. The more consistent you are with your content, the faster your brand will grow. The goal is to make yourself synonymous with your industry.

Share Content On a Regular Basis - In the early days of social media, the more you posted, the more engagement you could build up. Today, however, over-posting leads to boredome and annoyance. You want to keep the lines of communication open with your audience, but you also don't want to overshare so much that you look bold. A good amount of posts is around 3-4 times per week for individuals. As Michael Noice, founder of Entrepreneur Coach, explains, "A once-weekly Twitter post or monthly Instagram photo are not going to attain much, if anything. For this reason, its best to focus on two or three carefully chosen social networks and try to be active on them, rather than posting occasionally to a half-dozen." There will be days when you don't want post, and that's perfectly fine. Study the data associated with your posts and identify a pattern that works for you. If you're having trouble finding content to share and want more insight into what's popular among users, try searching via hashtag on Twitter, using news aggregator sites like Feedly, or signing up for Google Alerts.

Give high-value assets for free - See the demand in your industry and create assets to address those demands. It can be a piece of software or a free report solving some specific need or query in your industry. After creating it, give it away for free on your blog in exchange for the prospect's email. This way you will be seen as an expert who does not hold back on giving value first. Doing this pulls all the critical levers in building an epic personal brand.

Focus on SEO - SEO is a great way to get qualified organic traffic to your blog. This traffic will consist of people actively looking to get information in your industry and thus qualify as high-value leads. If you can be the person who addresses their needs, they will start seeking you or your content for further advice. This will build your personal brand effectively for that niche. To execute this perfectly, you need to rank on the first page of Google (or any other search engine) and typically for the top 3-5 keywords in your niche. Doing this is a bit hard and can take a bit of time. Having said that there are a few growth hacks to rank faster for your content. Firstly, create epic content. By this I mean 10x the no.1 ranked article in your niche by adding more points, insights, creating relevant infographics and more. Aim for a minimum of 1900 words. Secondly, do not go for heavily competitive keywords in your niche. Instead, use long tail keywords. For example, if the main keyword in your industry is "Internet Marketing", then focus on a long tail keyword like "Internet Marketing for Freelancers" or "Internet Marketing for Home Based Entrepreneurs". The goal is to find keywords with high traffic volume but low competition.

Build a list - Build an email list. Give consistent value to your email list members. Nothing is more personal than being inside someone's inbox. Take advantage of it and make them into your brand evangelists. First, drive traffic to your site. Then once the traffic is on your site, ask them to submit their email IDs in exchange for some awesome content (lead magnet or content upgrade). Once they sign up, win their hearts by delivering exclusive top quality content not available anywhere else. Consistently giving value at a place where you are seen almost every day is a great way to engineer an awesome personal brand.

Import Your Contacts - You might be amazed to see how many people you already know on the social media networks you're using. There may be tens, or even hundreds, of people with whom you haven't yet connected with. Import your email contacts from Gmail or Outlook, or contacts from your phonebook, into your social networks to find out how many connections you're missing. Linkedin, Instagram, Facebook and Twitter all allow for a free import of a certain number of contacts.

Keep it Positive - You now know some of the things you should be doing on social media to build the best social impression for yourself, but do you know what not to do to keep that impression a positive one? Think of your social media interactions and content creation as part of a resume of your work and a reflection of your professional attitude and overall personality. Avoid inflammatory religious or racial comments, and be careful when making political commentary that others may consider offensive. If you have concerns about not being able to voice your opinions to the extent you wish, consider creating two sets of social media accounts: one for private use (say whatever you want), and one for personal use (in which your responses and shares are heavily calculated). Keep your personal pages private to just close friends and family, and use your professional accounts to build new connections and career opportunities.

Grow your social media audience (organic) - Start putting dedicated efforts every day to grow your social media audience. Focus on channels where your target audience hangs out the most and start putting high-quality content which helps them. Here are the exact steps to follow.

- Start by joining Facebook and LinkedIn groups related to your industry.

- Post exceptional quality content which helps the members of the group. Be consistent in your posting. Do not pitch anything. Once the members of the group notice your content, they will visit your profile.

- Put a link to your own group and other social media profiles on your bio or cover image.

- Take connections to the next level by connecting with other members through your personal FB/LinkedIn profile.

Over time you will build up an audience that will start associating you with your niche, thus forming stepping stones towards a robust personal brand.

Be omnipresent online - Be visible everywhere, be it your blog, admissible social media channels and other primary platforms in your corporation - both online and offline. The more present you are, the more sticky your message will become. Also, this is a good way to take advantage of the mere exposure effect which is a psychological circumstance where people prefer things familiar to them.. You will start building up a niche follower based on experienced people ambitious about your industry. You will become their favourite source for all things related to your field.

Get into new social media channels fast - Get into new and uncharted social media channels fast. You will have a higher chance of becoming an influencer there as there will be very less competition.

Repurpose your content like a pro - Remodel your existing content across different content channels like Medium and LinkedIn. Use your existing article and record a video of you speaking about it, upload the video to Youtube and audio as a podcast. Also, ONE interesting way of standing out with your content in 2019 is by making infographics. Make an infographic out of your article using a clean design tool like Visme.co. Search Engines love Infographics because they simplify big intricated ideas into visually compelling and easy to understand images. It increases a visitor's time on your site and also rises chances of your content being shared in the community. All this adds great karma points to your brand reputation. So take your present content and add more modes of delivery to it.

Get a vanity URL - Get vanity URLs for all social media channels. The URL should either be your name/ your name + your niche / reflective of your niche. Do not play around much with it. Don't go artsy with fancy names that have nothing to do with your industry. Stick to basics and connect the name to an industry keyword. This will be great for making the audience see a connection between you and your industry. Also, this will be great for Social Media organic search optimization.

Find & Join Groups - Facebook and LinkedIn both offer thousands of opportunities to join groups focused on specific industries or topics. Use the search bar on each network to find groups that are linked to your specific area of expertise, then you'll be able to share your insights and build authority around your personal brand. Keep in mind that industry groups may be overcrowded with your competitors, so smaller, topic-based groups may be more fruitful in terms of reaching your audience. Once you're a member of your preferred social media groups, don't be afraid to jump into discussions and add your unique insights. It can be difficult to remember sometimes that that's what social media is all about. So don't be afraid to have conversations. If you simply join a group and don't participate, you won't gain any of the benefits listed above. On the other hand, showing that you're responsive will help you build your personal brand in larger communities beyond your own.

Build a Facebook Group to propel your personal branding - Apart from building a list, FB groups are another way to build a constant relationship with your target audience. Simply start an FB group in your niche, and provide consistent value to your group members through high-quality content. Solve their problems, talk about the latest trends, share the latest hacks and tools, do everything to win their confidence. The more value you provide, the more your target audience will see you as a leader in your industry. Building your personal brand on Facebook goes a long way as this is where people spend most of their time. The key is to focus on groups, not on business pages.

Ask questions - Humans are social animals. We love to share and tell stories. Hence everyone loves a good listener. A primary way to build a relationship with your email list and FB group is by asking questions. This will help you get critical insights and also build a rapport with strangers.

Keep Your Brand Voice, Image & Tone Consistent - You've probably already figured out that sticking to your defined persona is important. If a popular political commentator suddenly and radically switched parties, no doubt he or she would lose a lot of fans overnight. You must also remain consistent with your ideas and the ways you present them so that you're memorable and trustworthy. Dining the tone of voice that works best for your brand may entail some trial and error, but there are personal branding guides you can use to determine the best fit for you. It's not as easy as saying "I want to be funny," you need to further develop your ideas to support your approach. Following your brand guidelines helps to control people's perceptions. You can damage an otherwise flawless reputation if one of your profiles shows up with content or images that don't match up with your brand's voice.

Network with influencers - Start expanding your network by connecting with other members of the industry on Social Media. Type your industry keywords on Facebook and LinkedIn and join all the top groups which come up as results. Once there, start giving real value without an intention to sell. This way you will be seen as a valuable member of the community and not an annoying salesperson. Your ultimate aim should be to give so much value that your name becomes synonymous with everything good about your industry. Reach out to them with a "value-first" mindset. Provide them value upfront by giving your core service for free. Now I know the word "free" can make some of us frown. But when you do it to build relationships with people who are the stalwarts of your industry, then this free work will pay itself off in no time and skyrocket your growth. Just imagine a great video testimonial about your work from the biggest influencer in your industry Or an influencer blasting a mail to his 100k strong list recommending your work. You see the value now? Connect with influencers using networking tools like Meet Leonard or Duxsoup. These tools will help you send automatic connection requests to industry filtered members on LinkedIn. For finding email IDs of influencers, you can use a tool like FindThatLead. Another way to connect with influencers is by joining their courses/paid mastermind groups. Once a part of the group, provide upfront value to all the members to get on the radar of the influencer.

Get on major media platforms - List the top magazines, podcasts, TV shows, YouTube channels in your niche and approach them to feature you. You can pitch them to have you as a guest panelist, contributor, columnist or them doing a story on you. To do this right, you need to first build relationships with these platforms. Use the same value-first mindset and offer your help or something of high value for free. Once you get their attention, pitch them to feature you on their platform. Show them the value you can offer to their audiences with proven results of your work. Once accepted, give actionable value and do not hold back. The goal is to win the hearts of the platform's audiences. In the end, offer the audience a free cheatsheet or strategy call in exchange for them signing up for your newsletter. Add brand logos of all your media features on your website and social media profiles. Put pictures of your speaking gigs and TV appearances. This will build a lot of authority for your personal brand.

Document and showcase results - Results. They are by far the no.1 buying emotion, and hence the no.1 brand builder. Whenever you work for yourself or your clients, focus on documenting results. For example, if you are in the field of SEO, make it a point to screenshot your rankings for the targeted keyword. This will come as handy proof that you deliver on what you do. Likewise, if you work for your clients, make it a point in your contract that you are allowed to showcase the results you bring for them. Also, a very effective hack is getting video testimonials. When a number of your clients come on camera and share their success stories from working with you, your Personal Branding will skyrocket immediately. One of the world's leading consultants, Sam Ovens has more than 1000s of video testimonials on his site – consulting.com. Run paid ads on your video testimonials targeting potential clients.

Invest in paid ads - For all the amazing long-term benefits of organic traffic, we cannot deny that paid ads are the fastest way to reach your target audience. Use smart targeting hacks. Target people with an interest list of brand names only hardcore fans in the industry know about. The ad should offer something of value to your target audience and show your knowledge on the subject. Retarget the visitors of your site with a lucrative offer. Creating a personal brand on social media isn't easy. It requires a lot of thought and research to do successfully. It is not about what you look like or where you live, it's about what you stand for and what people should expect when they see you've posted a new piece of content. Think long-term and remember to take note of what's working and not working and adjust as necessary.

Why They Should Want You And Not Another Brand?

The world is full of brands. There are more than 200 million small businesses in the World, and even more mid- to large-size businesses that boost that number further. Even if only a fraction of those businesses challenge with yours, that's a great number to deal with in an age where information is plentiful and digital exchanges are commonplace.

To make matters even more arduous, all those brands are competing with one other for visibility by using marketing and advertising campaigns to clamor for their target audience's attention. If you want any hope of your own audience noticing your brand among this mass of competition, you need to make something to stant out from others . But how can you do that? By making sure your brand has, and shows these seven important qualities:

Originality - First, your brand needs to be original. If you attempt to mimic a competitor's brand, people won't have a compelling reason to choose you instead of that other brand. If your messaging relies on clichés and sales talk, it's not going to resonate with any of your customers. Instead, find an angle that nobody has taken before, and develop an image and voice that are wholly your own. This is easier said than done, of course, but it's a necessary step if you don't want to blend in with the competition.

Sincerity - Next, your brand needs to demonstrate a degree of sincerity. If you respond to all your customers on social media with the same copied and pasted corporate response, people are going to see you as a soulless machine that cares only about turning a profit. Instead, show your human side. Invest in the "personality" of your brand, and speak to customers the way you would speak to a friend. You might make some mistakes along the way, but your customers will be able to forge much better relationships with you in the long run.

Understanding - The best and most popular brands are the ones that understand their target audiences. They demonstrate this by creating messaging that is relevant for only one target niche; for example, if you're targeting parents, you might mention a common parenting problem, like having difficulty with a morning routine. This will demonstrate a degree of sympathy and instantly make it easier for that audience to connect with you. In time, this will lead to increased interactions with your brand, which in turn will lead to more traffic and conversions. Make sure you research your target demographics thoroughly and on an ongoing basis, and adjust your wording and targeting as needed.

Boldness - In branding, risk often leads to reward. The boldest brands aren't afraid to experiment with new techniques, or take a stance on controversial issues within the industry. They're somewhat polarizing, which means they could alienate a portion of their audience, but they also encourage more loyalty and respect from the people who stick around, and they never run the risk of being seen as "boring" or "just another brand."

Consistency - It's easy to blend in as white noise if your messaging isn't consistent. If your brand standards aren't clearly defined, or you have multiple people executing those standards to varying degrees of effectiveness, you might end up alienating your audience. The goal is to get your followers and readers to stick around as long as possible; but to do that, you need to give them a sense of familiarity and predictability. The best way to secure those qualities is to lock down your brand standards early on, and ensure that all team members working on your campaigns are skilled at their execution.

Visibility - Obviously, if people aren't seeing your brand, they won't be able to respond to it in any way. Though some potential customers will undoubtedly trickle in through organic searches and other inbound routes, the only way to build your reputation from scratch is to make your brand as visible as possible. Leverage different opportunities to diversify your strategy; for example, you might post content on external publications to build your reputation, launch a social media strategy or invest heavily in advertising and promoted materials. The bottom line is that you need some medium to promote your messaging -- otherwise, it won't matter how appealing that messaging is. For help getting visibility for your brand, see How to Get Media Exposure for Your Startup: The

Value - Brands can also stand out by offering more value than their competitors; that can be done in a number of different ways. First, you could simply offer better products and services; if you offer a similarly valuable product for half the price, it will be only a matter of time before people start flocking to you. Unfortunately, most brands don't have the flexibility to get this competitive (without eating into profits). Instead, you might offer value in terms of better, more informative content, or a stronger dedication to personalized customer service. Originality plays a role here, too, so think carefully about how best to appeal to your customers. If you're just starting to build a brand, these factors should guide you in its development. If you have a brand already, and it seems lacking, consider implementing a rebranding campaign, or at least adjusting your execution of your brand standards to reflect these values. At the very least, take the time to audit your current brand strategy and evaluate your adherence to the standards you originally set.

Without a strong brand at the foundation of your campaigns, you'll just be more white noise to the average consumer.

Content Marketing

Content marketing is the contrary of advertising. It's about captivating consumers with the stuff they really want, in a way that serves your brand's purposes and ideals, rather than just trying to jam your logo into their periphery. It's reaching the exact consumers you desire instead of a vaguely defined demo. It's to provide an experience they want, instead of trying to distract them from the one they came for. In short, it is the very evolution of advertising itself into something more effective, more capabale, and much less abhorrent.

Content Marketing isn't also a ploy that you can just turn on and off and hope that it will be fortunate. It has to be a mentality that is embraced and encouraged. Content Marketing embodies an organization's core brand components. It uses a collection of media formats such as text, video, photographs, audio, presentations, e-books and infographics to tell your brand or company's story. It can be read and checked on a variety of devices including computers, tablets, smartphones and others. It's distributed via owned, third party and social media platforms and it provides measurable results through the use of convenient calls-to-action and advertising codes.

A winning strategy succeeds when technology and people work together. Automation and semantics can help to filter, facilitate and uncover hidden treasures, but it is the human touch – thoughtful selection and consideration of content – that will create a truly new and engaging brand experience for audiences to discover, enjoy and share. In this sense Content Marketing is a winning strategy.

Content Marketing isn't push marketing, in which messages are sprayed out at groups of consumers. Rather, it's a pull strategy – it's the marketing of attraction. It's being there when consumers need you and seek you out with relevant, educational, helpful, compelling, engaging, and sometimes entertaining information.

The definition of content marketing further depends on the author's viewpoint and background, but the rules of good content marketing and essential strategies and principles are very much alike in most cases. One of the key similarities in all the different ways of looking at content marketing is that the customer experience and the needs, preferences and questions of people and the so-called target audiences are at the center.

A consistent use of relevant content runs like a thread through all marketing activities. Good content is essential everywhere so using it in a smart way is key too. Content marketing is a narrative form of marketing that provides customers with useful information, at moments when they are interested in receiving it, in an engaging, not "salesey" way. This enables it to break through the advertising clutter that consumers ignore or view skeptically, while it gently persuades prospects and helps buyers and the public.

Even if Content Marketing may appear to be a recent innovation in marketing practice, really it's simply a new technique to convey the same information that consumers have always wanted about products and services. Its power has been exponentially improved with today's social media platforms and other devices.

Business Objectives Of Content Marketing

There are numerous reasons why companies apply content marketing solutions. Basically, these reasons are the same as in the case of any other marketing practice. It does not come as a surprise that practically every company aims at winning customers (or maintaining the existing ones) and, as a result, at increasing the sales of its products and services. All actions within marketing are focused on this very objective. Content marketing is no exception.

However, if we assume that generating income is the objective, we will easily come to the conclusion that this objective is too obvious and too general. In particular in the context of the budget of the marketing actions, you must be perfectly aware of what the money is spent on and what effect you can expect. Precisely defined objectives will come in handy.

The major objectives of the marketers who decide to fire content marketing are as follows:

- Increasing brand information

- Lead a generation

- Converting force   into customers

- Building relation

- Customer confinement

- Website service

- Marketing

Depending on the approach, the objectives can be designated more or less accurately. Some marketers agree that generating leads and converting them into customers are completely different things. However there is more truth in the opinions of those who simply reduce the objectives to three categories:

- Rising sales

- Customer faithfulness

- Brand appreciation

This list seems familiar, does it not? After all, everybody wants to sell a lot and be identified within the industry. Here the key question arises – if the objectives and leads are the same as the ones of the traditional marketing, then why content marketing?

No need to look for the answer. Traditional methods do not always correspond to the real needs of the businesses. If you carried out a survey checking which of the above marketing objectives are not important for the company, you would learn that, regardless of the industry, company and market size or the turnover, everybody wants to sell and be recognized. This is what we know. We also know that if several companies try to win the customer, this is quite a challenge.

Bombarding customers with advertising content is

becoming less and less effective. The human brain becomes resilient not only to the number of outdoor messages, but also the more or less classic forms of display. There are more and more advertisements, but the number of them noticed by us is dropping.

As customers, we also rebel against spamming (as we see it) in spaces, whether public (a lot of cities introduce restrains on outdoor advertising, especially in the tourist-attractive district) or private (filters blocking the ads in the internet browsers is a standard) with such messages. Yet after all, the marketer wants the best for all of us. They just want to let us know about a new chance which we could possibly miss . Like a hundred other marketers in a hundred other corporations.

As a result, the classic marketing often turns out to be ineffective, or at least inadequate. In principle, it focuses on the direct message put in front of the customer, which is in the way . It aims at stopping them in their tracks even for a moment and forcing them to react to the offer. While reading e-mails from our colleagues, we need to filter the promotions, and while visiting our favorite websites, we must look for the content among the threatening banners. Can it work correctly?

Inbound marketing is an alternative – it is based on the assumption that the customers will come to me themselves and get interested in what I offer, if I provide them with an interesting content. Instead of irritating them and often misleading by manipulation with the ad, I make them find me themselves. And it works best if I am able to offer them the access to what they are currently interested in and what they need.

It is difficult not to deem this approach ambitious, as effective implementation of content marketing is truly an art. However, the market enforces such actions and for some time they have already been a standard for many companies.

Extra Benefits Of Using Content Marketing

More inbound approach - Content marketing is one of the tools of inbound marketing. As we mentioned above, it is a situation where a company strives to draw the attention of potential customers by providing them with quality content. These actions are effective only after some time, as it is not easy to build one loyal group of recipients who we can expect to buy our product. Nevertheless, the companies applying the inbound solutions are considered as places where the real experts of the industry work. What comes with it is that the customers are more willing to spend their money on organization which they perceive as professional. For the customer, the very moment of "getting to know" the company and its offer is much more pleasant, as it comes without the hard sell. Building the company image based on inbound marketing is surely an action worth dedicating some time.

Customer engagement and innovation - A customer interested in the given subject is an engaged customer. Logically, any person reached by content marketing must be interested in the subject which the content relates to. Interest does not mean already a potential purchase, but one person who voluntarily sub-scribes to the company blog is a more valuable lead than a hundred recipients of e-mailing. If our recipients regularly read the contents which we provide, then in their eyes we are the experts and innovators of the industry. This is often decisive when it comes to a purchasing decision. The reach achieved by whisper marketing is an extra gain. People who frequently take part in webinars that we organize, will sooner or later tell their friends about it. Meanwhile, it is hard to count on the recipient of our e-mailing or brochures to become our ambassador.

Development of knowledge culture - Despite many critical voices referring to what can be found on the Internet, there is no doubt that if it had not been for the global network, we would have not become a learning society. The demand for constant development of our skills is enshrined in our times more than ever before. As it is often informal (school, university or trainings are not enough), the global network is an obvious medium. You can find knowledge in any field here. While applying the content marketing strategies, we become a part of this culture of knowledge as its very important elements – the creators. It is difficult to measure how much this contribution is reflected in the business, but it is equally difficult to underestimate the chance that we get this way in the business of the 21st century.

Better use of company resources - In many organizations, knowledge about tools as well as resources are wasted. Companies often prepare data for industry reports, but do not always have an idea of how this data can be used beyond the in-company circulation. Meanwhile, if it is properly processed and described, it can constitute a perfect and – most importantly – required white paper. Others willingly apply the tools in video conferences and they do not realize that often a tool used for the purposes of in-company meetings can be useful also as an online seminar tool.

The conclusion is that we can make a better use of our knowledge and other resources which we already possess and which in big part have not been used so far. The argument for this kind of use will convince everyone – lower operating costs and a better marketing effect. It cannot be assumed straight away that content marketing allows creating "something" out of "nothing", but the preparation and launch of a campaign in a way forces us to analyze the resources and think about what we can get out of them and what extra costs we will need to incur. This way quite a few managers who were convinced that they perfectly knew their company discovered completely new areas.

Content Marketing Tools and Tactics

As you already know, Content Marketing is a marketing tactic using knowledge and experience of the company to advertise its products or services. After the lecture of chapter three you already know what the goals of content marketing are and what purpose it is for. In this chapter you will see what tools may be used to accomplish these goals.

Generally, each content marketing tactic has different objectives to achieve but basically we can indicate the following factors:

- To connect on the social web and company's website;

- To ensure quality and endurance;

- To have a past view of the marketing strategy you should apply;

- To answer the question how your content fills the expectations of your customer;

- To lead and manage online content;

- To create, unite and distribute content.

Those tactics help to provide better content, and you must remember that the better content the more visible your product/service is. The importance of Content Marketing and its tools is acknowledged by many researches. According to Content Marketing Institute, 91% of marketers use content marketing. Content Marketing tools are a real heart of this new marketing technique, and it is really critical to know exactly the function of each tool and what you can gain using each ones.

Audio Content

Audio is the Achilles heel of webinars, as well as other forms of content - like podcasts, teleseminars, and videos - that rely on clear sound. When you think of content, a majority of marketers think visually-based products, like blog posts, whitepapers, infographics, videos, and other interactive content. However, audio-based content is seeing a rise in popularity, specifically with the resurgence of the podcast. For those who aren't hip with the latest millennial trends, podcasts are digital audio files that discuss a predetermined topic and are usually available as a series, which are released to subscribers in installments online.

How popular are podcasts? Over 57 million Americans listened to podcasts in the past month, and that number continues to grow. It's clear that the resurgence of podcasts is not a passing fad, but rather a unique way to approach and deliver content to an ever-growing audience of highly educated and affluent users. Innovative marketers are beginning to tap into this demographic by creating podcasts of their own. To help you decide if podcasts should become a component of your content marketing strategy, here's a look at the benefits they can offer your business, as well as a few examples of successful business podcasts.

Here are a few of the advantages that developing a company podcast can offer your business:

Help Develop the Authoritative Presence of Your Brand. One of the top benefits a business podcast provides is the further development of the authoritative presence of your brand. The same way whitepapers and blog posts work to establish your brand as a thought leader and authoritative source in your industry, podcasts do as well. Creating a podcast that touches on the topics and trends that are important and relevant to your consumers builds trust, from the consumer's perspective, that you are an expert on the topic. This leads consumers to trust the opinion, advice, and content provided by your business, which can be used to boost conversions and improve customer retention.

Expand Your Audience Reach. Creating a podcast for your business greatly expands your current audience reach. This is because audio-based content in the form of a podcast introduces your business to an entirely new kind of audience. Podcast subscribers tend to be highly educated and affluent, according to The Podcast Consumer 2019 study by Edison Research. These are consumers that other means of content typically can't reach, meaning there is greater potential for leads and conversions from new consumers through a podcast than through a blog post. The market for podcasts is also less saturated with competitors, which means the consumers you're targeting have a better chance of discovering your podcast content organically.

Boost Brand Awareness and Loyalty. By implementing podcasts into your content marketing strategy and regularly posting them, your business also boosts brand awareness and loyalty among consumers. Your business podcast serves as an advertisement of your expertise and in-depth knowledge on various subjects related to your industry and can highlight various products or services you offer. By consuming this content, listeners become more familiar with your business and more loyal since you provide them with something they need. This helps to improve customer retention rates and boost conversions driven by customer referrals to your business.

Affordability and Simplicity. As with any other digital marketing strategy, ROI is an important aspect to consider before pursuing new types of content marketing. Podcasts are not only simple and easy to create, but they are also affordable. All you need is a computer, microphone, and an interesting topic in order to create a podcast. Minimal investment needed for the creation of your company podcast means more net revenue, which is always good for business.

In addition to that, podcasts are simple and easy to create, which means you can pump out more quality content in less time. Rather than having gaps throughout the week while your content writers are writing the next blog post or whitepaper, you can easily supplement this with a podcast. This allows your business to have constant content creation, which means higher search engine rankings and better odds your target audience will find your content organically.

Struggling to determine what a successful podcast entails? Here are a few widely successful podcasts from businesses and brands to give you some inspiration for your own version:

HubSpot's The Growth Show: HubSpot, the well-known inbound marketing and sales software company, launched their own podcast called "The Growth Show." This podcast's target audience is business leaders looking to grow their companies. The weekly show covers everything the audience wants to hear, from topics on growing a company to growing a team. Tuning in to a few shows is a great way to learn how an effective podcast is made, a few best practices concerning podcasts, and how to effectively cover topics for a niche market.

TEDTalks Audio Podcasts: Almost everyone knows and loves TEDTalks. The insightful and impactful video lectures created by TED, whose motto is "Ideas worth spreading," have gone viral and educated the public on topics ranging from the future of money to the importance of strangeness. Rather that having these lectures solely available in a visual format, the forward-thinking business has also made them available in audio podcasts. This has expanded the reach of their content and allowed them to connect with listeners who prefer the audio format, furthering the awareness of their brand and authoritative reputation.

VaynerMedia's #AskGaryVee: Another great example of taking visual content and repurposing it for audio-only consumption is the CEO of VaynerMedia's podcast, entitled #AskGaryVee. This is an excellent example of an interactive podcast that engages the audience by taking questions from listeners on marketing, entrepreneurship, and social media and having Gary Vaynerchuk, the CEO of VaynerMedia, answer them. Originally made for YouTube, the content has now been repurposed and reformatted for audio-only consumption which has helped expand the audience reach and boost attraction. If your business is already developing video-based content, repurposing it for audio-only consumption in the form of a podcast is an excellent way to expand the reach of that content.

As podcasts continuously grows in popularity, more and more businesses will begin to offer their own branded podcast in an attempt to tap into the enviable demographic that primarily consumes this content. Incorporating a podcast into your content marketing strategy is a cost-effective way to help expand the authoritative presence of your business, expand your current audience reach, and boost brand awareness and loyalty.

Video Content

Content marketing in its truest form is nothing but the production and online distribution of content that is educational slash informative in nature. The purpose of this content is to convert online content consumers into prospects/customers. And also to provide the current costumers with enough information and convince them to become repeat buyers.

Content marketing is used across many channels, with the help of different types of content. Which means it is not restricted only to text and video, it's a big part of it. Since video is a strong and effective way to spread your marketing message, it can take your content marketing efforts to another level. But once again, this depends on how well you develop your video content marketing campaign. And what you want to get from it.

Reasons Why You Need Video Content Marketing

By now you should know what video content marketing exactly is and how it's growing extremely fast. It's a stratagem that your business needs to incorporate in order to get a higher return from your online marketing efforts. Let's now look into a few good reasons as to why you should invest in video content marketing and make it a part of your core business strategy.

More Conversions - When it comes to running an online marketing campaign, the ultimate metric that matters is the conversion rate. Because if you're not converting your prospects into leads or customers, your business isn't growing, it's as simple as that. By leveraging video content marketing, you'll be able to get more people to sign up for your newsletter or buy your latest product. When compared to other types of content, video content can give your prospects the needed clarity to make the final decision. It gives you a certain edge over the competition and since quality video isn't as easy to produce, it can take a while before others catch up with you. A recent research conducted shows that 71% of marketers have found video content more conversion-friendly. When done right, it can easily help you get better results with minimal efforts.

Better Emotional Connection - If you look around the social media landscape, you'll find that videos are being shared the most in comparison to other content types. While there are many reasons as to why people like sharing videos, one of the strongest "why" is that people connect to the right video content on an emotional level. By creating videos that appeal to the emotions of your target audience, you not only give them a reason to consume your content but also spread it across their own network. For example, if you look at a traditional blog post, you won't find the emotional cues that come with video content. Right from the tone of voice to the sound effects/music being used, everything can have a positive impact on the viewer. Which ultimately makes your content stand out from the rest and also memorable. When interested people watch your video that evokes their strongest emotions (happiness, awe, anger, etc.), it may not push them towards taking action immediately. However, it will help them make a buying decision later on when they see more such content from you. So whether you are in the B2B or the B2C market, impressing the emotions of your audience with video marketing, can and will help you bring in more business.

Higher Accessibility - Let's face it, video production is no longer the difficult task it used to be a few years ago. You no longer need to spend a ton of time on creating a video or have a huge budget to achieve studio level quality. Yes, we're talking about video content that only the big guys were able to produce before. Thanks to the advancement in technology and with new/innovative tools available, creating and launching your own video has become much more affordable. In fact, it will keep getting easier in the coming years as more and more businesses jump into producing their own videos and starting their own channels.

Stronger Engagement Levels - Many studies have proven that visual content works great when it comes to engaging your target audience. People today like to consume to content that is visually appealing and engrossing. Now, this isn't limited to pictures or photographs. Video content is proven to be a big part of the "visual content" movement. With more and more people watching video content on social media sites such as YouTube, Facebook and Twitter, you can see firsthand how video is helping generate strong engagement from target users. When you create and share video content with your social followers, you have a 10X chance of them engaging with your video, which often translates to more shares and comments. However, do keep in mind that the quality of video content marketing matters to a huge extent and has a direct impact on the kind of results you are able to generate.

Easier SEO Results - Does video content marketing have an impact on SEO? Can videos actually help you rank higher in the search engines for keywords that are hard to rank for? The answer is yes, given that you're doing it right. There is little doubt that Google and other major search engines like Bing love video content and won't hesitate to rank it higher than traditional articles. According to a study done by Comscore, by adding video content to your site, you have a 53% higher chance to end up on the first page of the SERPS. This just goes on to show that quality video content can make a big difference to not only your conversion rate, but also the organic search traffic you generate.

If you want your video content marketing to deliver results, then you need to take a calculated approach to it. You can't just blindly play the video marketing game and expect to see returns. Here are seven important tips to help you make the most out of your video content marketing efforts.

1: Grab their Attention fast

Internet users are not as collected as they used to be. Today, it's all about finding the good piece of content. So don't be surprised if people jump your video to look for another one if they don't find it exiting enough. The solution is to attract your viewers without wasting their time and delivering on your promise. You only have a few moments to entice them less than 10 to be precise. So have an interesting, relevant start to the video and don't wait too long to reach the purpose. Whether your video is long or short, give your viewers a motive to watch it without skipping it.

2: Deliver Real Value

Creative video content marketing is all about giving immense value to the viewer in whatever form you choose. Your content strategy should focus on adding value to the lives of your target Public . How you add this value is subjective. Because what's valuable for your audience may not be that valuable for a different type of public. So for example, if you find that you can give profit by creating and publishing entertaining yet informative video content, do that. Or if you want to choose an even simpler path by creating videos offering specific (niche or industry related) knowledge, even that's fine. Keep in mind that any video that you develop must be watchable and enjoyable. Because if it is a drag, then it's not valuable.

3: Go Beyond YouTube

While there is no doubt that your video content marketing plan cannot be complete without YouTube and it's vital it is not enough. Basically there are many other valuable video sharing channels/platforms that you can tap into besides YouTube. Your goal is to reach out to your target audience in the best possible way, and that can't happen if you only focus on YouTube. The most obvious reason as to why you need to consider other platforms is because of the potential to connect with a different audience. For instance, the kind of people you can reach with your videos on Facebook is not surely the same as YouTube. Because Facebook users discover video content in a different way using different tools in between. Also, different platforms developed have people from various age groups using them. This is why it makes sense to leverage as many video platforms as you can. However, designate the majority of your time to a platform where your target audience is most likely to be found.

4: Stay Consistent in Your Approach

Consistency plays a big role in making your video stand out from the competition. Why? Because videos are visual, which means you're not limited in how you present the content. With every video you create, you can help your viewers resonate with your message by being consistent. Your brand's personality, look and design matters to a great extent in keeping consistency high. For example, if you are creating videos with people in them, then keep using the same cast so that your viewers see faces they're already familiar with. Similarly, if your videos only have a voice-over, see to it that the colors and the design in the video you use stay consistent. You may also want to plan your video content well in advance (create a video content calendar) to make sure your consistent with timing as well. However, when it comes to video platforms, your videos need to be customized for each. The one size/look fits all approach doesn't work here. If you're posting a video on

Instagram, then it helps to create videos that look more natural, unedited or spontaneous. But on YouTube and Facebook, people expect a professional feel, so that's what you give them.

5: Don't Ignore the quality Aspect

Just because you are creating and uploading videos on YouTube or Facebook doesn't mean that you should forget about quality. In fact, keeping up with quality is extremely important on these social media sites because they're moderated by real communities. Users won't think twice before giving your videos a thumbs down if they don't see quality. So say no to low-definition video and hello to HD video content that people like to view and share with others. As video platforms improve in quality and service, they expect to give their users a better experience. Which will only happen if you stop testing the patience of your viewers with bad videos. Remember, quality over quantity is the number one rule of creating amazing video content.

6: Optimize for Silence

Besides YouTube, other social media platforms such as Facebook, Twitter and Instagram tend to auto-play videos without sound. The user may or may not choose to watch

106

the video with sound. But stats show that up to 85% of videos viewed on Facebook are watched with volume down to zero. The simple reason for the "silence revolution" in the online video world (especially on social media) is that people are increasingly watching videos on their mobile devices. Since the social experience is largely silent, especially with people around, it's no wonder that many users prefer to viewing videos with sound turned off. So how do you impress users when they are only watching and not listening? By creating attractive yet relevant visuals that make the video feel engrossing. If there's dialogue in your video, then add English subtitles. In short, have sound in your video but also optimize for silence.

7: Add a Call to Action

What's the use of video content marketing if there's no actual call to action in place? Businesswise, if you're investing in video content marketing, then you need appropriate results. Having a clear CTA makes real business sense and it should not be put aside. Call to actions in videos need to be convoluted . Simply encouraging viewers to visite your website or subscribing to your newsletter at the end of the video is usually enough. But if you want to go a step higher you may have a call to action come up right in the middle of the video when the viewer is deeply engrossed in the video.

Writing Content

When you look for content marketing, you probably think of blog posts. But they're just one of the many types of content that can help you establish your brand as a thought leader in your industry and attract new forces. By diversifying the types of content that you share, you attract virtual people with different needs. Let us consider the types you absolutely need in your content marketing strategy.

Blog Posts - Blogging may seem like an outdated practice – but that couldn't be further from the truth. Blogs are not only a powerful tool for creating trust with potential customers, but there's another important group that reads blogs: search engines. Your ideal customer will find your blog when they research content that relates to you and your business, and Google will read your blog to get a true sense of what your website is all about so that it can recommend your business in its rankings to those same researching customers. Blogs need to be updated constantly, they cannot remain a static portion of your website, like say, the 'About' page. Further, they need to be about a specific topic to direct those leads to your brand. Riverbed Marketing is an inbound marketing agency, so I don't write blogs about Star Wars, or how well the Blue Jays did in the playoffs. Those topics would bring me plenty of Jedi and bat-flip fans, but the keyword ranking that helps search engines link customers to applicable content wouldn't allow me to educate prospective clients and share information about my products and services. So not only does blogging increase your site traffic – but it gets you better traffic. How? It custom tailors the audience you bring to your site so you attract the one's who are justifiably more inclined to do business with you. They're also a forever tool, meaning that once you click publish, that blog post is out there for good. It does not expire, or reduce in value over time – like PPC for example; turn off the money tap and the leads stop coming, too. Need to hear all of this in another way to convince you to hit the keyboard more often? 80% of daily blog visits are new, and receive 5X more traffic than blogs that post weekly. And, more blogs spell more traffic. You can generate 54% more traffic to your site once you've accumulated as little as 50 blog posts, according to Social Marketing Writing. Blogs should be at least 1500 words in length, according to quicksprout. Longer blog posts amounting to over 1500 words receive 63% more tweets and 27% more Facebook likes than shorter ones. 1500+ word blogs also achieve more SEO backlinks.

White papers - Case studies are designed to illustrate positive affirmations related to the inclusion or adoption of your business' offerings. They are compelling before-and-after overviews of your customer's interactions with your products or service. They provide confirmation that an investment – of either time or money – is a good call. We're naturally drawn to stories as a species, and case studies satisfy our basic need for a happy ending. They're also integral to speeding up the decision to buy. Case studies help cater consumer behavior into smaller, quicker modes of thinking – because there's a lot of information out there already and customers are happy to cut through the pages and pages of copy to find out if the decision to purchase has been a good one for people like them. The case study is a great way to quickly show how your company was able to solve a problem facing your targeted market. Good experiences read well to buyers seeking similar results.

Guides - Writing guides is a great way to build authority as an expert firm on a chosen field in such a way that stimulates both education and rationality. When you're able to help your market learn, they'll continually have faith in you. For example, maybe you're a catering company – why not write a few guides for readers about the different culinary neighborhoods in your city? Provide tips for getting a table at the new local hotspot; offer ordering tips, introduce the chef as a budding entrepreneur your company has respect for, and offer insight on the up-and-coming trends in the next big emerging food district. This gives your business the credibility to be trusted as savvy professionals and a strong presence in the arena. Guides allow your readers to understand you're in the know – further, they can outline multiple segments within a large topic. If you're writing about how great the foodie scene is in your city, you can touch on seafood, late-night, brunch, and mixology – all in one read. Writing guides can boost your company as a laid-back expert, inspiring this expectation from your readers; the next time they have a question, they'll be back for more info time and time again.

eBooks - If you have a need to communicate complex information in an intellectually stimulating way – ebooks are probably going to be a big part of your content marketing strategy. They're proficient in combining both rationality and practicality in a package that is geared at convincing your prospective customer you're the answer for their brand issues. Compared to other forms of content marketing, eBooks are extremely research heavy, relying on third-party statistics, and illustrations or visuals to help differentiate from whitepapers. Ebooks are also great ways to assist your SEO efforts, as their content is searchable and lends well to keyword research. In the scope of the inbound methodology, eBooks are great at seizing the customers attention during the convert stage. Hubspot tells us that eBooks are not only critical tools for nurturing your existing leads into more sales-ready positions, but they help feed your list of new contacts. In order to write a compelling eBook, you've got to bring a few different skillsets to the table. Journalism, design know-how, strategy, and project management all play a part in writing a good eBook - but don't fret - you can do it.

Infographics - Content marketing isn't just the written word. Infographics, which visually interpret data, appeal to visual learners. Not everyone loves reading content, and many people prefer to digest it in another format. If you've got rather dry data, turning it into an infographic is a great strategy for getting people to give a crap.

Guest Blog Posts - While these can cover the same topics and styles you used in number one, you'll be writing them for other blogs. By publishing content on other established blogs, you can expand your brand's reach. Just keep in mind: guest blogging works better if you establish long-term relationships and contribute regularly on the sites that are sending you traffic. Implement one or more of these content marketing strategies into your existing efforts and see if you can't expand your reach.

How To Choose The Right Platform

Many of the best social media platforms for business, like Facebook and Instagram, have become essential tools in the modernized marketer's toolbox. More and more public is using these channels to find new companies and engage with their favorite brands. However, most companies can't be everywhere at once, especially small businesses with stricht marketing budgets. That's why it's vital for businesses to be strategic about which social media platforms they work to build a character on. The key to successful social media marketing will be choosing the best social media platform for your career. This is based on a number of reasons including the type of business you have, what audience you are trying to reach, your specific goals, and much more.

Below, I've developed a quick and simple guide to choosing the best social media for business.

Instagram

Instagram is a staple of many small businesses' marketing campaigns. And for good reason. It has a large and diverse audience that is happy to engage with brands, resulting in high engagement overall. Research and case studies have demonstrated these benefits clearly, finding that they can translate directly into sales and leads.

Consider that:

- 80% of users follow at least one brand on Instagram, with 60% of these users saying they've discovered new products or services through this unique platform.

- At least 30% of Instagram users have purchased products they seen advertised on Instagram.

- 65% of top-performing Instagram posts clearly shows products.

People are happy to follow brands on Instagram, and they're actively discovering and purchasing products on the platform. That's a big win. Also worth noting is Instagram's continued efforts to embrace commerce. Instagram ads see excellent results and offer high engagement. Shopping on Instagram streamlines the Instagram sales process. And business profiles with over 10,000 Instagram followers gain "Swipe Up" links they can add to Instagram Stories to drive traffic directly to the site, something that was otherwise difficult to do on the platform. The platform keeps expanding, making it more valuable to merchants and ecommerce businesses, especially if they have products with a strong visual appeal.

Optimizing Your Instagram Profile

Most merchants know the basics about setting up an online profile; you need to fill out your contact information, have a keyword-optimized description, and choose a profile picture that's easily identifiable, like a logo. This is a great start.

But Instagram has rolled out several changes that affect business accounts. To get the most out of your limited Instagram profile space, you should include the following:

Clickable hashtags. These can now be added to your profile description just by entering # and then the desired phrase, just as you would on a post. Focusing on your branded hashtag is a good choice for most businesses.

Clickable profile links. There's several options for how to use this, but you can now also add clickable links to other user profiles in your own Instagram bio. If you have two different profiles for a sister company, you can use this to direct traffic there. If you're hosting a contest with another merchant, link to them when discussing the contest in your bio. You can also use this feature to send people to your personal profile if that fits with your branding.

Story Highlights. We'll talk more about Story Highlights a few sections down, but this feature lets you add "expired" Stories to different featured categories, which will be listed above your Instagram feed on your profile. This helps your profile to look fleshed out and allows you to showcase certain key Instagram content like UGC or posts that highlight your brand's story.

The Different Types Of Hashtags You Should Be Using

In order to fully expand your reach and get the most results from your Instagram marketing, you need to be using the right types of hashtags. There are six key types of hashtags that are crucial for ecommerce businesses to incorporate into their marketing strategy.

Branded hashtags: More and more brands will and should have a unique branded hashtag. They'll attach this to each post, place it in their profile, and persuade users to attach it to any posts in which they're sharing user-generated content. It may include your brand name, but it doesn't have to.

Contest hashtags: These hashtags are a type of branded hashtag created for a singular contest. These are often used to identify contest entries for photo submission contests, and to generate contest awareness overall. Furthermore, to the main branded hashtag contest, you should also incorporate general contest hashtags.

General appeal hashtags: There are certain hashtags that are popular among large, diverse audiences. These can help you get significant reach on your posts, because they're more likely to be sought out.

Niche-specific hashtags: Each industry will have phrases and keywords that are relevant only to their target audience. These hashtags won't get you the same reach as the general-appeal hashtags, but they'll get you more relevant traffic, such as #harrypotter (if you're selling jewelry inspired by the Harry Potter series).

Timely hashtags: Ongoing events and seasonal holidays can make great hashtags, especially when you factor in selling-focused holidays like Valentine's Day or Christmas. People are likely to be searching for content that's relevant at the moment, so take advantage of a few hashtags.

Entertaining hashtags: These will not help you with reach, but they will serve to entertain your audience and help you to establish your brand. They're meant purely to be funny or clever, and that is it. In many cases, entertaining hashtags might be grouped together, one after another, to tell a story.

For best results, do research on each of these hashtags, and use a variety of combinations of different hashtags in each category for your posts. This will strengthen your branding while helping you to reach the largest and most relevant audience possible.

Hashtag Best Practices

Hashtag usage is one of the most significant factors that will determine your success on Instagram, and they're unsurprisingly a little difficult to crack. Fortunately, the following best practices will help you maximize your reach and your results:

- Include your branded hashtag on your profile.

- List any entertaining hashtags at the very beginning of your hashtag list, where they're most likely to be read.

119

- Use a considerable number of hashtags. The limit is max 30 hashtags per post. However, numerous case studies have found that somewhere between 9 to 11 hashtags for each post will be the sweet spot, especially if you classify the types of hashtags.

- Switch up your hashtags. Don't use the same hashtags on every post. Create groups of hashtags that you can cycle through for different posts. Not only will this increase your visibility to different audiences, it can also keep your account from being flagged as spammy by Instagram.

- Take time to explore each hashtag. This can help you discover new hashtags to target, and ensure that you don't accidentally use a banned hashtag or jump in on a topic without knowing what it means.

Instagram Stories

Instagram Stories started out as an add-on feature borrowed from Snapchat: a way to share short-lived photos and videos that disappear in 24 hours with your followers. But it's developed into an essential part of the platform. Stories led to Story ads, and now Instagram has given us Highlights so that our Stories can live on forever. Let's take a look at how to use them.

There are a variety of strategies that you can use to get results from Instagram Stories, each of which will benefit your business in different ways.

Share content created by your audience. You can use Stories to showcase user-generated content, which is always a crowd-pleaser. Your followers love to see that you care enough about them and their content to feature it on your site. It also saves you from having to create the content yourself, and acts as powerful social proof.

Acquire content from your audience. Stories can also help you obtain UGC, which can happen in several different ways. You can place calls to action for users to share pictures of their latest purchase. You can also use poll stickers to get feedback and generate immediate social proof.

Share moments from events. Your Stories are also a great place to cover and promote events, whether they're several weeks away, happening right now, or from the past. This is a great way to provoke FOMO and show everyone what they're missing out on, which can build brand awareness and increase attendance.

Be authentic. Instagram Stories are quirkier than feed content, so it's a great place to showcase your fun side. Use images and videos to tell your brand's story, throwing in some behind-the-scenes content when possible.

Go live. Instagram Stories allows you to broadcast live right from your mobile phone, and your followers can engage in real time. You can host q&As, talk about a specific topic, or interview a featured guest or influencer. Once the live is over, you can have it set to be played with the rest of your Stories.

Extending The Lifespan Of Stories With Highlights

Realistically , stories would disappear after 24 hours just like the Snapchat feature they were emulating. Instagram recognized that this was resulting in lost ROI on that content, and gave us the opportunity to create highlights. Highlights exist on our profile page, and we can add stories to them after their 24 hours have passed. You can create multiple highlights for the best effect, using one for user-generated content, one for brand storytelling, and one for your events. This helps users to find content they're looking for when they first come to your profile, which can help them get to know you and trust you a little faster. To insert highlights to your profile, click on the icon with the black + above your gallery. You'll need to give a name your highlight and select the stories you want to add to it. You can play around them at any time.

Instagram TV

All marketers know that developing a strong presence on social media is crutial for their business, so using Instagram TV to further promote your brand sounds like a no-brainer. With IGTV, you also get to jump on board sooner and get a head start on your competitors. Unlike most other new platforms, your reach won't be limited to just a few thousand early adopters. As explained above, all Instagram users can install and use Instagram TV with their known accounts. This surely means that your videos could potentially reach more than a billion users from the get-go.

What's more, if a user starts following your channel, your videos will play automatically as soon as they launch the app. That way, your message could reach millions of users without a single dollar invested in Instagram advertising. Instead, you can use some of the marketing money you save to produce high-quality content for the platform and reach an even wider audience.

Although IGTV is still in its early stages, there are already plenty of great ways you can use it to bring your brand closer to audiences, improve its reputation, and attract new clients as a result. Here are five ideas that could help you get your Instagram TV channel up and running.

Broadcast Live Videos. Until now, the only way to broadcast live videos on Instagram was to use the Instagram Live feature. However, those videos would only be available to your followers and would expire after 24 hours. With Instagram TV, your live videos will remain available on your channel indefinitely. You can use this format to broadcast live q'n'A sessions or transmit interesting live events. What's more, IGTV allows you to upload your videos to Facebook Watch, so your content will be available on both platforms at once.

Repurpose Your Content. With IGTV and the new audience it allows you to reach, all your old content can become new again. Take your old horizontal videos, edit them to fit the new vertical format, and post them on your IGTV channel. If you run a podcast, rather than sharing teasers and asking followers to visit your website to listen to the latest episode, you can post full episodes to your IGTV channel and accompany them with interesting visuals. This is much more convenient as it allows users to listen to your podcast without leaving the app.

Make Your Videos Instructional. Instructional content is always popular and doesn't have an expiration date. With IGTV, you can take your "how-to" videos to a whole new level by allowing followers to replicate what you're doing in real time. Whether you're focusing on cooking, do-it-yourself home repairs, beauty and makeup, or fitness, the 60-minute format gives you plenty of opportunities to create captivating evergreen content.

Rerun Your Best Instagram Stories. If you're investing a lot of time and effort into creating engaging Instagram stories, you probably want to preserve them and give them time to reach new audiences. With Instagram TV, you can now compile all your favorite stories into short videos broadcast on your channel. If you use Stories a lot, you can do periodic digest-style videos where you would include all your stories posted within a certain timeframe.

Create Your Own IGTV Original Series. In many ways, IGTV works like actual television, so you can also use it as such. We already mentioned sharing your audio-only podcasts on your Instagram TV channel. If this proves a hit with your followers, you could use a camera to simultaneously record a video version of the podcast and post it exclusively to your channel. Similarly, you can create your own weekly or biweekly IGTV show where you would introduce your products and services, answer your followers' questions, and chat with interesting guests.

Although Instagram TV doesn't yet allow advertising, there are many ways you can use it to bring your brand, products, or services closer to audiences worldwide. With more than a billion users and less competition than other, more established social media apps, IGTV is an excellent platform for marketers looking to attract new customers with engaging, creative content.

How Instagram Advertising Works

Since 2015 anyone can now learn how to create Instagram ads through Facebook's self-serve advertising platform. With it, you have total power over your ads, how they appear, and who sees them. And not likely sponsored posts and paid partnerships, your ads get posted directly from your own account. The advantages to this method of Instagram advertising include:

- Ascendable pricing.

- Self-serve and quick

- STRONG reporting so you're in control.

- Highly refined public targeting.

What's more, with Instagram's move away from a chronological feed in favor of a well curated feed, you never know how many of your followers will see your posts.

Types of Instagram Ads

Photo Ads - A Photo Ad is one simple photo in landscape or square format. These are the simplest in terms of visual asset needs, since you just need a single image. Here's an example of a Photo Ad from outdoor ecommerce brand Fimbulvetr Snowshoes, which takes users to the product page of the snowshoe featured in the ad creative.

Video Ads - Instagram used to have a 15-second limit for videos, but it has since lifted that rule. Now, videos can be up to 60 seconds long and shot in landscape or square format. Dollar Shave Club uses the Video Ad format in its Instagram advertising to promote a new membership deal, highlighting the various products included in the deal.

Carousel Ads - An Instagram Carousel Ad can have anywhere from two to ten images and/or videos that users can view by swiping through. West Elm uses Carousel Ads to highlight their range of products for their Instagram advertising campaigns.

Slideshow Ads - Slideshow Ads are similar to video ads in that they appear as a video in users' feeds. These ads, however, are made up of a series of still images which play as a video, much like a slideshow. You can add text and audio to your Slideshow Ads.

Stories Ads - Instagram Stories Ads is one of the newest kinds of ads available to businesses on the platform. Instagram Stories is similar to Snapchat in that it allows users, and brands, to share self-destructing photos and videos. Brands can also advertise on Instagram Stories with photo or video content. Online fashion brand ASOS has used Instagram Stories Ads with much success to build brand awareness and ad recall.

Facebook

If you would like your business to have a presence on social media, Facebook is probably one of the first social media platform you think of. More than 1.4 billion people use Facebook every single day, and multiple times a day. It is almost certain that your potential customers are on Facebook and using it actively to engage with their family, their friends, and their favorite brands.

Whether you're running a brick and a mortar store, an

ecommerce site, an agency, or a software company, you can use Facebook for adverstise your business. In this guide, I hope to cover everything you should know to put your business on Facebook, to market your business, and to gather your results. The good news is you don't need a budget of Super Bowl proportions to get into this type of game. Sharing valuable content that help you connecting with fans and potential customers is your most reliabale play. For example, 93% of social media advertisers use Facebook ads, which clearly suggests that it's surely worth the while.And if you find that statistic motivating, I've compiled nine more helpful data points below to help inform your strategy and take your Facebook business to the next level.

1. 37% of Facebook users say that they follow Facebook Business Pages because they want to receive special offers. Offering those who follow your Facebook Page estimated offers will help motivate your target audience to smash that "Like" button. This tactic works for businesses both large and small.

2. A post's average organic reach is only around 6.6% of the Page's total likes. There was a marketing-world rumor that this reach only extended to an average of 2% of the page's total likes, but in actuality it's more like 6.6%. While having a high number of likes on your Page is important, the Facebook users who like your Page won't do the work for you - you need to produce engaging posts, no matter how many likes you have. The more you understand about how to generate engagement through your posts, the better.

3. 49% of Facebook users only access the site through the mobile app. That means that almost half of all Facebook users see your ads on their phones. Additionally, mobile app fans are arguably the more frequent users, as they have Facebook right in their pocket 24/7 rather than just when they can access a desktop computer. You know what that means? Your content needs to be mobile-optimized. In addition to making sure any landing pages your ads point to are mobile-ready, consider posting more vertical photo and video content, and keep long-form posts easy to read, limiting the use of the "read more" button.

4. One study says that the most effective length for Facebook ad titles is four words, with 15-word link descriptions. While there's definitely a time and place for long-form content, your Facebook ads and link descriptions apparently aren't it. If those four words in the title, plus a bit more info in the link description, can elicit FOMO (fear of missing out) and draw the reader in, even better. Don't overshare here, you want a high CTR after all.

5. Videos with auto-playing sound annoy 80% of users. Most of us scroll through our Facebook feed in public - on the subway, in class, or waiting in line at the grocery store. Ironically, these places each include about a dozen people who will definitely give you a dirty look when an ad pops up and starts sounding off immediately. Because of this, you need to consider that the majority of your ad viewers are going to be consuming with sound off, so ensure that you include relevant subtitles and visual queues to lessen the need for audio.

6. Videos with closed captions increase viewing time by about 15%. Reiterating the point above - closed captions will prompt viewers to stick around longer. This way, Facebook users can still watch and understand your videos, no matter where they might be.

7. Your video ad has about three seconds to capture viewer attention. Three seconds sounds like nothing, but your video has a ton of opportunity to pack a punch in that small amount of time. Similar to post titles, ensure the first three seconds of your video are informative, but mostly full of FOMO. A bit of suspense, or the idea that your video isn't revealing everything right away will give your viewers incentive to keep watching.

8. Shorter posts get about 23% more interaction than long Facebook posts. Keep it short and simple. Again, your audience is likely consuming on the go, so you need to get their attention fast and smoothly and trust that your subsequent landing page will hold their interest beyond that.

9. Video posts get more attention therefore shares than any other post type. This is another exceptional reason to incorporate video content into your Facebook marketing strategy - the average video share count is about 89.5 shares.

Facebook offers convincing opportunities for businesses, but also significant challenges. Hopefully these clues will point you in the right direction to help you drive better results from your Facebook marketing efforts in 2019.

Facebook Organic Reach

Before we move any further, let's take a step back and give a definition, in case you are not familiar with the meaning . In general, natural reach is the number of users who will see on their screens what you posted, with $0 spent on your side. On the other hand, paid reach includes the users who see your content as a result of paid promotions and advertisement . In our case, the number of users that your content from your profile gets is the number of your Facebook organic reach.

Tip 1: Publish more content that your fans actually want to see. Many public pages just publish once a week but I recommend posting a variety of content styles over the week. Optimal post reach can be received just once or twice a day. You can line up the posts for the week in facebook scheduler to see what kind of content people react to. Check your insights to see what people most engage with and start forming a list to keep you on track for 2019.

Tip 2: Create a dialogue with people who may see your content by including a more enticing comment on your post. This is done by asking questions or telling a story. You can even say something observed about the image or video you're posting about. I'm giving you a ton of awesome examples and specific instructions for you to get that engagement popping today on the podcast.

Tip 3: Do you know who you're speaking to? Look at the people who follow your page and engage with your posts by going to their page and reading what they post about. You can also learn alot about your fans in comments. If you spend the majority of your time speaking with people on each post, then the post does much better and you can utilize your time more wisely by commenting and sharing additional things right on comments. Insights is also a great place to see how your posts performed. Listen to today's podcast episode to find out how to use this information to start posting smarter content.

Tip 4: Post Micro content that doesn't link off the site. This is anything that condenses your content and keeps people in the feed. Think of how you scroll though the newsfeed and think about what you engage with. People don't trust links as much as they used to and often they don't want to leave a social media page to consume it so try to design the majority of your content be consumed right on the social media page. For instance: publish a video trailer that promotes your youtube videos rather than always just sharing your YouTube videos on the page. You can still share a youtube video so it plays on the page but publishing directly to Facebook will definitely give your music a boost into the newsfeed.

Tip 5: There are so many mistakes that people make on facebook but here are some of the worst page killers. Posting the same link and photo's over again. Not answering comments at all of fast enough. Always be social and active. Never let a comment go unanswered for more than a few hours. I like to stay on a social media page for 30 minutes after posting so I can give attention to my first responders. Those first responders are your super fans so don't leave them hanging. Make sure you answer those comments. Ignoring messanger. Don't let that be your dead zone. That's where you can capture your audience onto email lists, nurture more supportive relationships and make sales. Stop linking off of facebook.

Tip 6: Be consistent: Many people give up way too quickly. They post a few time and then stop. Facebook knows how much time you spend on the app so when you post and leave, they are actually least likely to show your content to the majority of your followers. Posting regularly and staying on the app to engage with people in the newsfeed, answer comments on previous posts, and being present on messenger tells the app that you're an active user. All this activity boosts your posts and helps to qualify your account. Facebook also gives more credibility to the next post you publish after a successful post so try not maintain consistency and don't stop posting once you have achieved some reach and activity.

Tip 7: The best posts to try on facebook: live stream on facebook, post video directly to facebook, images without links, selfies, statements and quotes, funny memes, questions, polls, and trending or popular videos shared on facebook. Look at trending posts on facebook for possible topics of conversation that could improve your engagement. This does require some trial and errors and make sure that your choice of topic aligns with your brand and page content.

Facebook Ads

There are lots of good reasons to invest both time and money into Facebook Ads. All those options they offer, while seemed to be overwhelming, also offer immense customization and creative control over your ads. For example Want to target vegan parents of young children near Soho? Want to target these individuals, but only if they're already connected to your Page or business? You can actually do both simultanously . The targeting and retargeting options available through Facebook Ads are incredibly developed .

Facebook Ads are also connected to Instagram Adverts. You can work both in a single campaign, connecting you to audiences on both platforms. Since the largest goal of

Facebook Ads is to put your content in front of users - without waiting for them to come find you, this is a great advantage. And while some people don't trust the cost of Facebook Ads, it's still pretty affordable compared to some alternatives, including Google AdWords. This is particularly true when your ad campaigns are given a high importance/value score, which means Facebook believes your ad is a good fit for your target audience, and they'll lower your CPC.

To fully harness the power Facebook has to offer, it is important to take into consideration the different ways that you can advertise on Facebook and when each approach is appropriate.

Boosted Posts: These engagement-boosting ads can be your daily go-to for any scenario. Did you know that the average percentage of your Facebook community that organically sees your daily content is 6.5% or even less? Facebook's algorithms cater content to show audiences what they prefer to see at first, but your content can get on that list. Belt this algorithm by putting a small budget ($10 - $30) behind your daily posts. You can select targeted audience to be people who like your page, making sure that this content will pop up in their feeds even if it is not something they often engage with.

Like Ads: If community growth is a primarily important for you in 2018, like ads are the perfect solution! These ads specialize in growing your community and generating more "likes" for your social media page. It gets even better when you consider you have the ability to select the exact public that you want to follow your brand. Select an age group, location, demographic, or interest to ensure that the new followers you receive will be engaged with your content and ultimately becoming brand advocates. We suggest spending anywhere from $300 to $2,000 a month on these ads.

Lead Ads: What if you could use Facebook to poll your audience on a daily basis and learn about their shopping places , preferences, and even question them about new product ideas? Well, forced ads make it possible to gather consumer intel like these examples and more. Instead of directing audiences to an external landing page to submit a form or survey, lead ads collect this same info through Facebook. Once the ad is clicked, audiences will be able to answer the questions asked and easily submit them in a matter of few seconds. An extra sweet feature to these ads is that Facebook automatically fills in any basic personal information (such as name, birthday, email address, etc.) saving users time and keeping audiences from navigating away before completing. When it comes to the right amount to spend, ask yourself: how much would you spend to get this sort of information from a specific group? The sky's your limit.

Conversion Ads: If you read my recent post on the Facebook Pixel, you know that conversion ads are another treat that I can't live without. These ads are perfect for tracking the success of a promotion and helping to see exactly how your landing pages are performing. If I notice a high amount of clicks on my ad but not many people submitting forms, I know that the landing page is not performing well, due to copy, design, or content. Through these ads, I am able to make changes mid-promotion to ensure that I gain as many submissions and/or leads as possible.

Before you dive into one of these advertising approaches, it's important to remember these Facebook advertising best practices. Once you've got these down, you'll be ready to harness the power of Facebook ads in your favor.

How To Set Up A Campaign

Creating high-converting Facebook Ads isn't actually as difficult as it sounds. Because many brands and small businesses prefer Facebook's Ads Manager to the more intricate Power Editor, I am going to use the Ads Manager's Create an Ad process for this Facebook Ads guide.

1. Develop Your Strategy First

Before you can even start looking at the Ads Manager, you need to have a strategy in place. Without this, you absolutely will get confused by all the options and you'll end up creating an ad campaign that doesn't actually target anyone useful because you're creating an ad for no one in particular.

For each campaign that you're going to create, you need to ask yourself:

- What product or services am I specifically promoting?

- Who am I targeting?

- Will they be a cold audience or a warm audience?

- How will they use the product?

- What is their pain point, and what objections will they have?

- Which stage of the funnel are they in exactly?

- What is the goal of the campaign?

- Do I want leads, brand awareness, site traffic, sales, or something else?

If you don't have a strategy with a goal of what you want to accomplish, you won't be able to create strong ads. Develop your game plan first.

2. Choose Your Objective

The very first thing you should do when creating your campaign is to choose your objective. It is important to choose the right one, because Facebook will optimize ad placements based on your objective of preference . In times the right objective can lower your CPC and improve your results. You can choose from the following objectives:

- Brand awareness

- Reach

- Traffic

- Engagement

- App installs

- Video views

- Lead generation

- Messages

- Conversions

- Catalogue Sales

- Store Visits

You want to select an objective that most cohesively aligns with your underlying goals. If, for example, you're running a video campaign that's designed to drive sales, choose the "conversions" option instead of the "video views" choice. Sure, you do want video views, but not at the expense of more conversions.

3. Target Your Audience

You should start making your ad campaign with a strong idea of who you want to target - now's your chance to flesh that out.

You can use:

- Custom audiences, which target specific users from your email list, or users who have taken certain actions on your site, your Facebook, or your Instagram's marketing profile.

- Lookalike audiences, which replicate qualities from your custom audience

- Demographic targeting

- Location targeting

- Interest/behavior targeting

- Connection targeting, which determines if you want your ads to be shown to users who are or are not connected with your brand

4. Choose Where You Want Your Ad To Be Displayed

Next, at the ad set level, you'll be choosing what placements, apps, and devices you want your ad to be shown on. You can choose mobile only, desktop only or both desktop and mobile. You'll also have multiple options on Facebook, several on Instagram, and the audience network. You can run ads with almost all placement options selected (unless you choose to run an Instagram Story Ad, in which case you can only use that placement), or you can disable or enable only certain ones. You can read an extensive resource on ad placements and their pros and cons here.

143

5. Set Your Budget

In the next section, you'll be able to choose your budget, schedule your ads, and select an optimization method. You can choose a lifetime budget or a daily budget and you can either have your ads run indefinitely or be scheduled to start and end on certain dates. You can even choose to use dayparting, which allows you to run your ads only at certain times or on certain days of the week. At this stage, you can also choose if you want to optimize your ads. For those who are wary of this, Facebook automatically has things set up for you and I'd only recommend going in and manually updating them if you're familiar with the platform and have reason for doing so. That being said, you can choose to change what you're bidding on (like link clicks or impressions), if you want to spend your ad budget as quickly as possible or spread it out over time, and if you want to set a cap on your bids.

6. Choose Your Ad Format

There are several incredible ad formats on Facebook. You can choose from:

- Single image ads

- Video ads

- Carousel ads, which allow you to show several videos and/or pictures

- Canvas ads

- Collections, which open up to be a full-screen mobile experience.

Each ad type as it's own unique benefits, but video ads and carousel ads (with or without video) typically have some of the highest engagement and CTR rates.

7. Don't Forget the Details

At the very bottom of the creative section, there's a lot of small details that are easy to miss. These include multiple sections where you can put copy, along with things like CTAs and URL descriptions. Take advantage of every single one of them. The CTA button will help drive conversions, and using the right copy in the right places will make a world of difference on your campaigns.

8. Monitor Your Ads Carefully

After you've started your campaigns, monitor them carefully. Some campaigns may start to see increases in CPC after the frequency gets too high and others may start out at a significantly higher CPC than you'd expect. Others may just not be performing the way you'd like. Facebook's Ads Manager will show you the details of all of your active campaigns. Watch the CPC, frequency, relevance scores, and number of actions taken particularly carefully. These are the most crucial metrics.

Create The Business Page

A Facebook Business Page is a free opportunity for businesses to increase brand awareness and generate sales on Facebook. To create a Facebook Business Page, simply log into your personal Facebook account, click "Create a Page" from the drop-down menu, and then follow the steps to build out your business profile.

Follow These Steps To Learn How To Create A Facebook Business Page:

1. Register for a Facebook Business Page

Facebook business pages are created using a personal Facebook account, so you'll need to first log in to your Facebook account. In the right-hand side of the blue toolbar, find and click the "Create" button. A drop-down list will appear after clicking "Create." Select the first option, "Page," to create your Facebook Business Page. You will have the option between two page categories—a "Business or Brand" or "Community or Public Figure." Most for-profit businesses will want to choose Business or Brand.

2. Enter Your Business Information

Tell Facebook what you want the name of your business page to be. This should be the same as your actual business name. Then, choose a business category that best represents what your business offers. For example, a clothing brand could enter "Clothing," which will then pre-populate a list of related options for you to choose from.

3. Upload Your Profile Picture & Cover Photo

Next, choose a photo to upload as your business page profile picture. Businesses commonly use their logo as a profile picture, but you may use any photo that represents your business and your business' branding. Be sure that your image is clear and doesn't get cropped. If you don't already have an image in mind that you'd like to use, or are in need of a new one, it's worth checking Fiverr. There you can find freelance experts who can design a professional profile picture for you, whether it's a logo another image, at an affordable price. Click here to browse freelancers.

Next, consider uploading a cover photo. A cover photo is the background image that appears on your Facebook Business Page, similar to your personal Facebook account. You want your cover photo to be visually appealing and representative of your business. Your cover photo should be at least 400 pixels wide by 150 pixels tall. If you are having trouble finding a cover image, you can create one for free using Canva. It includes many Facebook cover templates that you can easily customize without any graphic design skills or knowledge.

4. Invite Friends to Like Your Page

Facebook will prompt you to invite your current Facebook friends from your personal account to like your new business page. Existing Facebook friends can provide a good initial base of likes for a new Facebook Business Page, so it is advised to go ahead and do this. Either click the pop-up prompt, or invite friends from your "…" button from your business page as illustrated below.

5. Include Additional Business Details

In the left-hand menu, find and select "About." This is

where you will input information that tells readers about your business, from ways to contact you to your products or menu. Enter all pertinent information, such as your website, hours, and contact information. It's not uncommon for a business' Facebook page to rank higher in organic search than their website, given Facebook's domain authority. Keeping this in mind, it's important to complete all information, as it may be a potential customer's first point of reference for your business.

6. Add a Button to Your Page

After you have input all of your important information into your Facebook business page, you will want to add a button to your page, which will appear in the top right-hand of your business page below your cover photo. This acts as your Facebook page's call-to-action (CTA) and is free to use. Including a relevant one to your business can help generate more leads, and in return, increase sales. To do this, click the blue "+ Add a Button" option on the left-hand side of your page below your cover image. You can choose from the following types of buttons: Book with You, Contact You, Learn More, Shop, or Download. Select the button type that best suits your business. For example, a hair salon would likely want to use the Book with You option, whereas a brand selling products would find the Shop option a better fit.

7. Market Your Facebook Business Page by Being Active on Facebook

Creating a Facebook Business Page is only the first step to marketing your business on the platform of Facebook. You will need to be active on Facebook in order to market your page and grow an public . For example, you will not only want to be persistent in posting on your page, but you will also want to actively take part in relevant groups where your target audience is likely spending their time.

How to Grow Your Business with Your Facebook Business Page

For a Facebook business page to serve as an effective marketing channel for your business, you will need to promote your page. You can do this by taking advantage of Facebook opportunities from Facebook Ads to get your name out there by participating in relevant Facebook groups.

Here are different way you can get started promoting your Facebook Business Page:

Link Your Facebook Business Page to Your Website - Be sure your Facebook business page links to your website. You can do this a number of ways, from including your URL in the About section to adding a button to your page that links to your site. You can also post content on your page with links to your website.

Advertise on Facebook - Once you create a Facebook business page, you're all set to advertise on Facebook. Facebook advertising is not only an affordable advertising platform where you only pay for the clicks your ad receives, but it is also unique because you can target an extremely specific audience through sophisticated ad targeting. Your ads are shown to precisely the people you need to reach, giving you the opportunity to land in front of the right people. If you are producing great posts and content on your page, another option is to use Facebook Sponsored Posts, which is a form of advertising that will put your post in front of your target audience. It is a very easy and cost-effective way of having your Facebook posts reach users outside of your Facebook network.

Get Listed in Google's Organic Results - Ranking on the first page of Google search results can be difficult for small business websites. The good news is that having your business listed on Facebook (and other online directories like Yelp and Google My Business) increases your chance of your business ranking high in search results.

Market Your Business Online for Free - If done right, you can also see results from marketing your Facebook page without having to pay a dime. You can do this by sharing content like videos, blog posts, and images that will garner your audience's attention. We have an article on how to get free Facebook likes that will teach you what types of posts will get you more fans. If you own a seasonal shop like a food truck or pop-up shop, and you don't have a separate business website, you can also use your Facebook page as your main online presence.

Connect with Your Customers - When people like your page, you can tell them what's new with your business, share interesting articles you think they would enjoy, and respond to their posts on your page. Remember to regularly respond to comments and questions from your followers and build a relationship with them. This is a great platform for a local business that relies on local patrons to keep their business booming.

Build Awareness Through Facebook Groups - Facebook groups can be a great opportunity for businesses to increase their exposure and build brand awareness. Find relevant Facebook groups and actively participate in them. Keep in mind that your participation should generally be with the goal of connecting with new people and helping others, not offering a sales pitch, so refrain from using it as a platform for selling your product or service.

How to Optimize Your Facebook Business Page

Optimization involves changing one element of your Facebook page at a time to test the performance of the change. For example, you may change different aspects of your business page from your profile picture or cover photo to the type of call-to-action button you use. It's beneficial to optimize this way because it leads to higher engagement, following, and ultimately, sales.

Optimization also help your Facebook business page in the short-term as users are notified when you update your profile, making your page appear in their news feed. Gauge performance by tracking likes, views, and interactions of the posts you've optimized. For example, if your previous profile picture had 72 likes and 13 comments, but your new one gets 144 likes and 24 comments in its first month, you can assume the newer image is better. Another good way to do this is by using heatmap software to track how and where users engage on your Facebook business page. Hotjar is a great heatmap tool with a free forever plan that can be used to track what users do on your Facebook business page.

LinkedIn

With a rapidly growing user base of 500 million professionals, LinkedIn provides organizations with unique opportunities. Beyond being a prime place to share content and showcase thought leadership, LinkedIn performs almost 3 times better than Facebook or Twitter for generating visitor-to-lead conversions. Creating and maintaining an up-to-date LinkedIn Page is crucial for any marketing strategy. At a glance, running your LinkedIn Page might seem pretty simple. But growing an engaged following on LinkedIn is apples and oranges compared to any other social network. And given the platform's best practices and new slew of business features, there's perhaps no better time to revisit your LinkedIn presence for optimal engagement.

Below I have broken down the anatomy of the perfect LinkedIn Page whether you're looking to optimize your current profile or start from scratch.

Best Way To Set Up Linkedin Page

First things first: businesses need to cover the basics of their profiles. Although setting up your LinkedIn Page is straightforward, there are some important decisions to make in terms of optimizing your creatives and profile copy.

Choosing a logo and cover photo - Chances are you already have the creatives on deck for your logo and cover photo. In addition to your tagline, this is what users will see "above the fold" when checking out your business. Unlike Facebook or Twitter where you might use a cover photo of your team, clean and colorful imagery is your best bet on LinkedIn. When in doubt, keep it simple. The approach you take to your creatives is totally up to you, though I recommend coming up with a cover photo that's exclusive to LinkedIn for the sake of giving your profile some flavor.

Filling out your LinkedIn profile - Any given LinkedIn Page contains a series of subsections. Businesses should ideally fill all of these sections out 100%, with the exception of the "Jobs" section if you aren't hiring.

About - This section highlights your organization's basic information, including a brief "About" blurb and a place to list industry-specific keywords in the "Specialties" field. The information here is more akin to a Facebook "About" section versus a stylized Twitter or Instagram bio. Your LinkedIn "About" section highlights your company's mission statement as well as industry-specific keywords

Life - The "Life" section is an opportunity to show off your organization's culture. Here you can highlight your organization's values, provide a snapshot of your workers' day-to-day lives and explain what separates you from other organizations in your space. LinkedIn's "Life" section is the perfect place to highlight your company culture and values

Jobs - If you're hiring via LinkedIn, this section will aggregate and house your job listings. LinkedIn allows businesses to post job listings

People - The "People" tab will populate based on which workers have your organization listed as their employer. There's also a brief demographic breakdown based on your employees' location, education, roles and skills. This section is valuable for potential prospects and people interested in reaching out to your organization.

Best Practices To Maximize Your Linkedin Engagement

Now that you have an idea of how to fill out your LinkedIn Page and what to post, it's time to think about how you're going to maximize your profile's reach. Want more followers? Looking to attract the attention of industry players and influencers? Here's how you do it.

Get your employees involved - Okay, this is the big one. Employee advocacy is the absolute best way to grow your LinkedIn presence and exponentially increase your content's reach. Think about it. When you restrict your organization's content to your Page, you're only being seen by your current crop of followers. But let's say you have a few dozen employees with a couple hundred followers each. Even if there's some overlap between your page followers and theirs, this enables your posts to be seen by thousands who'd otherwise miss out on them. Rather than manually have employees post organization content, platforms such as Bambu or LinkedIn Elevate allow organizations to curate and amplify social content within a single platform. This encourages a uniform approach to sharing content that ensures that as many eyes are on your organization as possible. Bambu's employee advocacy platform makes it a cinch to share company content through individual profiles.

Prioritize video content - Video content is quickly taking over social media itself and LinkedIn is no different. LinkedIn released its video capabilities in 2017 and has been stressing the importance of video ever since. It's no surprise that video content is among the most popular and LinkedIn and appears to be prioritized by the platform's algorithm. From educational video to commercials, organizations should step up their video production ASAP in an effort to stand out on the platform.

Come up with a consistent content calendar - Based on our data regarding the best times to post on social media, good engagement appears to shift between mornings toward the late-afternoon throughout the workweek. It is not rare that we see most organizations post at least once daily, although we encourage businesses to experiment with frequency. Having an understanding of your timing and determination can help you put together a comprehensive content calendar specific to LinkedIn. With the help of Sprout, you can then publish directly to your LinkedIn Page and schedule your content alongside your other types of social profiles.

Stay tuned for opportunities to connect and engage - Whether your content strategy focuses on posing questions or sharing thought leadership, your public is expecting to hear from you. 55% of buyers say that liking or responding to a consumer's post on social media helps brands connect with consumers. Now with "real-time" notifications for comments in the Smart Inbox, it's easier to create connections with your consumers with more contentment . Think: shorter response times when cultivating conversations or answering questions directed towards your brand/business . Acting quickly in those moments inspires more engagement from your public.

Understand your analytics - According to Sprout's 2018 Social Index, audience insights and data-driven strategy should be the top priority of any organization looking to thrive on LinkedIn. In other words, you need robust analytics. What posts are your top performers? When are you scoring the most shares and followers?

LinkedIn Groups

The best way to place your company in front of your customers is to create a group that is relevant to your field. In this group, you can start discussions, and create an open forum for your customers to share their opinions,

159

suggestions and concerns. However, you cannot just create a group and leave it at that. You must actively participate in those discussions and address your customers's opinions or concerns.

Other than creating a brand new group, you can also consider joining other groups and communities that are related to your business's niche. This way you can listen to what your target audience is talking about and the kinds of problems they are facing. Address these problems in those groups and propose solutions that your company can offer. If you develop a connection with a potential customer in the group, you can send them a message via LinkedIn InMail and start building a stronger relationship with your customer.

Organic Growth

While you might understand the importance of an established LinkedIn company page for your business, it can be more difficult to determine what best practices to follow in order to grow your page organically. By employing these tactics, businesses everywhere can expect substantial increases in the value of their LinkedIn business pages:

1- You should make sure that all employees complete their profiles on LinkedIn and add your company to their profiles as employees are automatically followers of their Company Page.

2- Motivate your employees to share your content with their many connections. This will raise your brand perception and increase the engagement including the likes, comments, and shares. Remember that employees on average, have 10 times the connections as their company has followers on LinkedIn and so when they share your content with their connections, this will increase the popularity of your brand.

3- Follow other businesses and influencers in your industry and engage with them so that you can use their reach to grow your following as well.

4- Post updates consistently that your followers can like, share, and comment on. When they engage with your content, their followers will also see your own updates. According to LinkedIn, B2B prospects engage with 7 pieces of content on average before making a purchase .That's why Top performing Companies will post several pieces of content each week, and some even post daily. Content often published on LinkedIn include images, infographics, posts from the company blog, leads to events, webinars, ebooks, and many more. So drive higher quality leads by featuring a good mix of upper funnel and lower funnel content, including tip sheets, eBooks and case studies you should take in consideration.

5- You could Post high-quality Content. Your content should focus on teaching others how to solve a problem and establish you as a thought leader in that particular area. According to LinkedIn, 74% of prospects choose the company that was first to help them along their buyer's adventure. So sharing perspectives on industry news and trends, helpful product how-to's and articles that reflect your company's vision will definitely establish you as a though leader in your own industry.

6- Post and share rich media like engaging visuals, videos, and infographics that capture the audience's interest.Based to LinkedIn, adding rich media to your LinkedIn Sponsored Content can increase CTRs by as much as 39%!

7- Engage with your network by responding to comments, liking or sharing other posts, and engaging in relevant groups for your industry. Also, joining groups that are relevant to your target audience will enable you to know what your audience is talking about and communicate with them. You can also create groups to share your content that your audience will be interested in and demonstrate your expertise while at the same time ensure that no competitors get in.

8- Add social sharing buttons and links to your Company Page on your website and other social media platforms. Add them on all of your blog posts and website content to allow users to quickly share content as updates.

9- Update your Career Section frequently with job postings so that people looking for jobs will find your page in search features or through connection suggestions and will hopefully follow your Company Page to stay updated with new openings and future opportunities.

Paid Advertising

With LinkedIn Targeted Ads, you can target the right people at the right time with LinkedIn Advanced Targeting Features. LinkedIn targeting is unparalleled since it provides you with targeting options that aren't available in other social media platforms like Facebook. The

Demographic Targeting is exceptional where you can target people specifying the company name they work in, their job function, their seniority level, the industry they're operating in, the company size, the degrees they've acquired, the education level, the groups they've joined, and many more. This targeting method is what makes LinkedIn Advertising Cost higher than other platforms, but at the same time the leads acquired through LinkedIn Ads are more qualified and valuable leads which makes the Conversion Rate higher.

LinkedIn Dynamic Ads now available in the Campaign Manager are great to get new followers. LinkedIn Dynamic Ads are divided into three parts which are the Followers Ad, the Spotlight Ad, and the Content Ad. The Dynamic Followers Ad allow you to expand your page followers similar to Facebook Page Likes Ad, a new feature that wasn't available for us before.

Also, LinkedIn Sponsored Content helps you to publish relevant content and reach a targeted audience of professionals beyond just your LinkedIn Company Page Followers. You can promote and advertise the company's content through Sponsored Content Ads to target a niche audience, increase visitors and generate sales leads. You can also choose to add a "Follow button" to your Sponsored Content if your goal is actually to acquire followers.

You can also add a "Follow button plugin" for free to your website so people can follow your Company Page from your site. You can request the "Follow Company Plugin Generator" through this link.

Also, promote the company's content through other types of LinkedIn Ads like Text Ads, or Dynamic Ads to target specific audience and generate awareness, increase traffic, and generate qualified leads. Another type of Ad is Sponsored inMail where you send a personalized message to LinkedIn members' inMail box and with a CTA feature asking them either to subscribe, sign up, download, and many more.

Remember to identify your target public clearly and determine who you're trying to reach and who are the people you want to be your Company Page's Followers before starting your Ad Campaigns by answering the following questions:

- What is their job title and what are the functions?

- Where are they actually located?

- What industry do they work for ?

- What is their advantage ?

- What are they interested about ?

- What kinds of content they follow?

- What kinds of questions do they ask ?

- What are their weak points?

Youtube

When people talk about social media, they rarely mention anything about YouTube. This is sort of surprising since YouTube is the second ranked search engine of choice by volume actual used. Now, more than ever, YouTube users can up being just as valuable, if not more valuable, than traditional social media followers for the matter.

While the userbase makes up the heart and spirit of all social media platforms, a subscriber on YouTube is much more important than a follower on either Facebook or Twitter. Organic Facebook followers are much harder to reach than they used to be, and Twitter followers see a cascade of tweets by the hour, making it likely that your tweets go unnoticed. Unlike any other social network however, nearly 80% of adults consider themselves a "regular" systematic YouTube user. In addition, it is very easy to use, since a Gmail account is all someone needs to create their own playlists, vote on videos, use the comment system, or become a subscriber.

The ease of use, combined with the gift to create so many different social signals, makes YouTube an important part of any social network marketing strategy. These users are going to see your new videos, they are going to pay attention to the message in the videos, and they can even help attract new subscribers and also comment.

How to Create Videos for YouTube

Making videos that people enjoy can be challenging, especially if you are just starting out. Most people like to do things at their own speed, which makes it even more crutial that your video is good, or people will not want to waste their time with it. In a article from the Huffington Post, companies seeing the greatest YouTube success ranked different types of videos by their importance and effectiveness. Below, I cover these videos as ranked in the article.

Before you brainstorming for, filming, and editing your videos, take into consideration this list of video types.

Customer testimonials. Customer testimonials are short interviews with satisfied customers. Customer testimonials can help build company and product credibility.

On-demand product demonstration videos. Demonstration videos are short pieces of content showing the benefits and proper use of a specific product .

Explainer and tutorial videos. Explainer videos are in-depth videos explaining how to use a product or various parts of a certain product or service. Tutorials can be used to answer customer support questions or explain a new product feature and evidence the use of purposes of it.

Thought leader interviews. Interviews with experts or thought leaders can help deepen your company's credibility in an industry.

Project reviews and case studies. Project reviews or case studies revalueate a successful campaign or project and often include statistics and results.

YouTube Live. YouTube Live allows users to broadcast live content to viewers online . Live video allows you to easily share unfiltered moments and lets your audience participate with real-time comments and reactions with emoji. Live videos on YouTube are recorded and appear like any other video uploaded . To Go Live from your YouTube channel by clicking the camera+ icon in the top right corner and choosing "Go live".

Video blogs. Video blogs are daily or weekly videos documenting daily life or activities. You could also record a video that list or highlights a blog post so your audience has multiple ways to digest the content.

Event videos. Event videos feature in-person experiences at a conference or expo and can be a great way to show the excitement of a group.

How to Promote Your Videos

Once you have your first video ready to go, you need to promote in a proper or it may end up being completely unnoticed by the YouTube community. This can be done by:

Give it a good description – The title and description for your video can help bring in search traffic both on YouTube, and through search engines. This is incredibly important, especially when you are just starting out, since the value of an individual viewer or subscriber is much higher when there is a low number of them in the first place. Think about what people might be searching for and if your video would be a good fit for them. Throw a couple of those keywords into your title or description, and you should be ready to upload it.

Comment on related videos – While this might seem a little "spammy", it is still one of the best ways to get your video in front of a targeted audience. There is a good chance that if a viewer is interested in the video that you commented on, and it is at least somewhat relevant, they may be interested in yours as well. This is best done while your channel is still young and you do not have a lot of subscribers. Building up a healthy subscriber base is crucial to your success, and you will probably gain a few subscribers with this method. Doing it too often though, and doing it when you already have a fair amount of subscribers, will lead to diminishing returns.

Use your existing social media accounts to promote your videos – If your other social media accounts already have a decent number of followers, you can use your videos as posted content. This gives your other social media accounts some variety, since you are posting a video, and it will direct people already interested in your business or website to YouTube, where they may become subscribers there as well.

Keep people on your channel with in-video links – Having a link to another one of your videos come up when people are almost done watching their first video will keep people around longer. This increases the chance that they will perform an action which can cause your video to become more popular. They might become a subscriber, give it a thumbs up, or even share it off-site. The longer you keep someone engaged, which can be easy with an in-video link, the more valuable that person becomes to you.

For those of you starting out with YouTube, you will probably find that promoting your videos is going to be the hardest part. Over time, as long as you keep adding quality videos, it should become easier as your success starts to build upon itself. The most popular YouTube stars do not have to worry about how they are going to promote their videos, they are going to get hundreds of thousands, perhaps millions of views no matter what specifically because they are already wildly popular. You on the other hand will need to keep promotion in the forefront of your mind.

There are so many different ways that YouTube users can

increase your social media presence, and by extension your main website or business. You don't really see the same kind of versatility with other social networks, but the tradeoff is that you absolutely need to keep users engaged more than with just written content. If you make good videos, and you promote them the right way, you will probably have a lot of success building a YouTube following, which can end up giving you a big return on your social media budget.

Organic Growth

With so many subscribers, channels and viewers on the podium, increasing traffic on YouTube has become a challenge for brands. We've listed the following tips to boost organic reach of your YouTube videos.

1. Conduct thorough keyword research

YouTube's conclusion takes into account keywords in the channel description, video titles, video descriptions and tags. Ask yourself: what is my public searching for on YouTube? Now take that knowledge and research how your public is looking for that content. Are they typing in "How to" or looking for something more specific and detailed?

YouTube auto-suggest is a great place toto begin. Let's say your video is about styling ripped jeans. YouTube auto-suggest provides insights into what people constantly search and you can get a pretty good idea of what to title your video, too. You should also take a more analytical path to.

2. Optimize your videos (before and after uploading)

This is easily the most important part. Optimization is key to both before and after uploading to successfully increase views.

Tips for optimization before uploading

- Shoot high-quality video and use premium type editing

- Use a primary keyword to name your uploading file

Tips for optimization and filters uploading

- Write clear, natural titles with max 1-2 keywords

- Write titles no longer than 70 characters ca.

- Use high-volume, low-competition keywords in the descriptions

173

- Try to Keep video descriptions between 100-200 words, using a primary keyword throughout

- Upload a custom thumbnail to show off in search results

- Include relevant, on-topic video tagging

- Keep information natural to set realistic expectations for your viewers

3. Fill out the about section

Your company's YouTube profile section is prime real estate for not only telling your brand story and describing your channel, but also great place to implement market keywords. Fill in as much information as you can, including social profile links and your company website. You should also utilize keyword meta tags to describe your channel, which you can found under "Advanced" in channel settings. Channels with complete information stand out and rank higher.

4. Follow a consistent upload schedule

YouTube recognizes active channels, and the more videos you will upload, the stronger your channel will appear.

This might mean posting once or twice a week or maybe biweekly. Upload schedule should remain frequent and posting should happen when your particular audience is most active on the platform.

5. Find smart ways to engage your viewers

Lastly, find unique ways to attract your viewers to keep them engaged longer. As stated above, YouTube strongly ranks videos on whether or not people are watching them. High view rate and public retention are major factors in organic performance.

A few other tricks to keep your audience engaged:

- You should request that they subscribe

- You should Add end screens and cards to direct viewers to another video

- You may Organize videos into playlists

- You may also Hold engaging contests

Paid Advertising

Are you ready to develop your first ad but unsure on which format you should use? I am not surprised. There are three types of YouTube ads - all of which have their own requirements, benefits and also use cases.

Pre-Roll Video Ads - This type of YouTube video ad is shown before a video, and runs about 30 seconds. They're charged per click, meaning you only pay for the total number of clicks generated, rather than the number of video views. Since these ads are charged per-click, they're usually the most cost-effective for campaigns focused around on-site conversions such as link clicks or to grow your subscriber list.

In-Stream Ads - If you've selected TrueView ads to form the basis of your YouTube advertising campaign, your videos will be shown to users before they view a normal video. You'll be charged per view for these ads and there's no upper time limit.

But here's the catch: Whoever's viewing your ad has the opportunity to skip your video after five seconds. Although you've got more space to play with, you've got less chance of encouraging someone to watch the entire video, especially if the first five seconds don't grab their attention. That's why these ads are usually best for generating brand awareness.

176

Bumper Ads - If you don't fancy creating longer videos to promote via YouTube ads, don't worry. You're able to use the bumper ad format to show a six-second, non-skippable clip before a regular video:

You might not think that six seconds is enough time to grab your audience's attention when running video marketing campaigns on YouTube, but Google found just the opposite: in 300 bumper campaigns, 88% drove a significant lift in ad recall - making them a fantastic format to use if you're looking to boost brand awareness.

In-Display Ads - If you don't want to advertise within the video itself, in-display ads are your best bet. Charged on a per-view basis whenever someone clicks the link, in-display YouTube ads are shown on the right-hand side of a user's screen.

Despite the name, in-display ads aren't the most prominent type of YouTube ad. Users are able to bypass your advert altogether if they're only interested in watching the video they're currently viewing, but they're a good option if you're looking to boost conversion rates. The person who's clicked on your in-display ad has done so by choice, meaning that they're already interested, and therefore potentially easier to convert.

How to Produce the Perfect Creative for YouTube Ads

Now that you've selected the suitable YouTube advertising format for your product or service, it's time to think about the overall video, which is often referred to as one of the most important aspects of your entire campaign. Creating a video that's enjoyable to watch is the good basis of any successful YouTube video campaign. After all, you can't expect to see results if you aren't prompting people to listen to whatever you're saying.

Here's the list you'll need when nailing the creative of your video ad:

- Make the first 5-8 seconds alluring. After this point, people may decide if they want to skip your ad or continue watching.

- Replicate the language, cinematography and personality of the industry you're looking to advertise to so you can tailor and develop it to what they want.

- Design a thumbnail for your YouTube ad that fits this industry as well.

- Focus on explaining one key point to avoid annoyance within your viewers.

- Tell a story to attract your audience, but make sure it's relevant and fits within the time you've got.

Other Tips and Tricks

I have created a comprehensive YouTube marketing strategy 2019 including all the tips and tricks to ace YouTube marketing. Follow these tips to master the YouTube marketing strategy 2019:

1. Build your YouTube brand channel

Your YouTube channel should spin out your brand's story to the people. From your channel icon to channel description, everything should speak your brand's voice. Add your brand's logo to the YouTube channel icon. Add a custom YouTube banner as well, with social media icons leading your audience to your social media handles across platforms. In the 'About' section of your YouTube channel, add a brief description of your brand. Your description should introduce every new visitor to your brand and reflect your brand voice. Put calls to action leading to your website or any other pages you want to lead your audience to. Finally, divide your videos into different playlists. You can create branded playlists with names unique to your brand. Categorise playlists into webinars, behind the scenes etc., depending upon your video content.

2. Consistently create and add compelling videos to your channel

Create video content that gets your audience talking. Most importantly, use YouTube videos to bring out your brand's story.

Are you a B2B brand? You can create YouTube videos that complement your blog or website content. Bring your customers to give quick reviews of your brand. Ask them to share the experience of using your products, working with your brand and so on to take your YouTube marketing plan to the next level. Create and run a separate Video blog channel for your brand and interact with your audience using the platform regularly. Interview industry professionals, seniors and subject matter experts. Informative video content is most popular with the audiences. Post step by step videos and tutorials on how to use your products or services. At the same time, keep posting videos consistently on your channel. Find out the right time to post content, when the audience is most active on the platform. Add videos to your channel accordingly.

3. Leverage YouTube tools and features

YouTube has a host of tools and features that can help you enhance your YouTube marketing strategy 2019. Use end screens and cards to add your desired calls to action. Shared a video on how to assemble a product? Lead your audience to other videos on how to use the product and other similar content from your playlists. Add transcripts your videos. Make your video content universal by adding closed captions. It cuts out the language barrier and makes your content consumable by audiences across borders. At the same time, you can reach out to the disabled with this YouTube video feature. A keyword-optimized video transcript helps enhance your YouTube SEO as well. These incredible tools come as a part of your YouTube channel. Make the most of these, to level up on your YouTube Marketing strategy.

4. Optimise your YouTube video description and thumbnails

Since your YouTube video thumbnails and description are the ones that provide a glimpse into your content, optimize these for better results. Your YouTube thumbnail should push YouTube users to click and watch your video. The most important elements of a good YouTube thumbnail image include a picture and a caption. Add a popping image and caption that draws the attention of your audience. Use facial-closeups for best response. The idea is to create a visual representation of the video content in the thumbnail. Equally important in your YouTube marketing strategy 2019 is your video description. Make all your YouTube video descriptions keyword optimized to enhance YouTube SEO. Also, make sure that your YouTube video descriptions align and complement your YouTube video content. Apart from using keywords, use catchy phrases that push the users to hit the play button on your videos.

5. Add YouTube stories to your YouTube Marketing Strategy 2019

After Instagram and Facebook, YouTube hops on to the stories' bandwagon. YouTube now has the stories feature which allows for you to add short, mobile-only videos that expire after 7 days. YouTube offers this feature to creators with more than 10,000 subscribers on the platform. Easily create YouTube stories in a matter of seconds with the tap button on your profile and then edit them. Trim your YouTube stories and add filters, music, text, stickers, and even links to your videos. As a creator, this tool allows you to diversify on your content on the platform. With this new feature and the tools that come along with it, you can build a strong relationship with your community. It will also help you boost engagement. Create compelling stories that

182

generate interactions with viewers. Respond to all the comments and expand your community.

6. Optimize Video Titles For YouTube Voice Search

Enhance your YouTube SEO by optimizing title for YouTube voice search. People use YouTube voice search to find videos quickly, without having to use their fingers to type out the video titles. Since voice search is an easier, hassle free way to get YouTube video results, you need to ensure your videos appear before your audience.

Most importantly, optimize your YouTube video title to make it SEO friendly. Imagine yourself using YouTube voice search for your videos. Would you go for a longer YouTube video title or a shorter one? Most people will use a small number of keywords to describe their YouTube query. So, frame a YouTube title that includes important keywords, is short and simple and has a conversational tone. This will improve your YouTube SEO to a great extent and eventually increase your views on the platform.

7. Influencer Marketing On YouTube

Include Influencer marketing as a part of your YouTube marketing strategy 2019. There are 3 main important benefits of partnering with an Influencer:

- Access to a bigger audience

- Access to another person's skills

- Assortment of your content

And all these advantages add up to bring more engagement for your brand. Find out alcove Influencers. Someone whose niche may aligns with your brand. Using Unbox Social's social media analytics tool, impress different Influencers from your niche. The business feed feature on the tool dashboard allows you to track as many Influencers as you want and get regular updates about them. Monitor their activity and stay on one Influencer. Engage them and bring them on board. You can use Influencers to shunt great quality video content. Weight their content creation skills and influence to your best. Ask them to do product reviews, feature on your channel for account takeovers, or make them your brand agents. There are many ways in which you can use Influencer marketing as a part of your YouTube marketing plans . At the same time keep track of all the trends and watch out for outdated Influencer marketing practices that you may be nourishing in.

8. Use YouTube Ads

Paid content will continue to be an important part of a good YouTube strategy 2019. A sure way to make your videos appear before your audience is through the advertising option. YouTube Ads come in 6 different formats- skippable TrueView in-stream Ads, 6 second bumper Ads, sponsored cards, overlay Ads, display Ads and Trueview Discovery Ads which shows   on the homepage, alongside search results and next to related videos. If you aren't using YouTube Ads to market your brand, you may do it now and check out the results for yourself.

9. Monitor your Competitors

Monitoring your competitors is an essential part of every business and marketing strategy. Competitor analysis can easily be done by visiting their YouTube channel as well. Identify their videos with most views to identify content that most people engage with. Use that content to draw inspiration for future video posts. Skim through their comments to find out any mentions or naming of your brand. If you spot your brand mentions, make sure to respond to each of the comments. Also find out if any of their Ads are featuring on your videos. If that is the case, you may block these on the Google Ads manager.

10. Track and report on important metrics to learn from them

An important part of YouTube marketing strategy 2019 is

to track your performance and watch out for extensive metrics. You may Use a social media analytics and reporting tool such as Unbox Social. With this tool, you can track all important social media metrics and then generate customized reports of the same. Use Unbox Social to monitor metrics like watch time retention, top videos, video-wise engagement. Monitor your audience metrics along age, gender and even location. Target audience fragment accordingly.

11. Keep up with industry trends and updates

To be on top of your game in any industry, it is necessary to keep track of industry trends and updates. The social media industry is a potent one in itself. New features and trends in the Business as well as on the platform will inform your YouTube marketing plan. Use Unbox Social's personalized feeds to derive information and daily updates on your industry from your connections. Get an edge over the others by always staying on top of news, trends and updates in your business.

A great YouTube marketing technique involves leveraging all the tools and features at your disposal and employing them to build engagement. It also involves keeping watching on the industry as well as your competitors.